LESSONS FOR THE PROFESSIONAL ACTOR

For Zelda,
  Because you got the message —
      Much love,
          Joanna   6/3/62

LESSONS
FOR THE
PROFESSIONAL ACTOR

Michael Chekhov

from a collection of notes
transcribed and arranged by
Deirdre Hurst du Prey

introduction by
Mel Gordon

Performing Arts Journal Publications
New York

9 8 7 6 5 4

Distributed by The Johns Hopkins University Press
2715 North Charles Street, Baltimore, Maryland 21218-4363
www.press.jhu.edu

Library of Congress Cataloging in Publication Data
Lessons for the Professional Actor
Library of Congress Catalog Card No.: 85-60185
ISBN: 0-933826-79-6 (cloth)
ISBN: 0-933826-80-X (paper)

Design: Gautam Dasgupta
Printed in the United States of America

Publication of this book has been made possible in part by a grant from the National Endowment for the Arts, Washington, D.C., a federal agency, and public funds received from the New York State Council on the Arts.

A catalog record for this book is available from the British Library.

Contents

Preface

In November of 1941, Michael Chekhov was offered the opportunity of presenting the principles of his method to a group of actors who had attained professional standing in the New York theatre. They had been trained in diverse ways, some having worked with teachers of Stanislavsky's system, others with the techniques of Meyerhold and Vakhtangov, some with the Richard Boleslavsky-Maria Ouspenskaya school, while still others had trained more recently with Tamara Daykarhanova, Vera Soloviova, and Andrius Jilinsky. All were eager, hard-working actors who felt that Michael Chekhov's method would offer them a challenge and a fresh approach to the art of acting. Among the group were those who had seen Chekhov in brilliant performances with his Moscow Art Players in New York in 1935, playing leading roles in *The Inspector General*, *The Deluge*, and *An Evening of Anton Chekhov's Sketches*. Many had attended the lecture on "The Actor and the Theatre of Tomorrow," which he gave at that time at the New School for Social Research. Others had seen his Broadway productions of Dostoyevsky's *The Possessed* in 1939, and Shakespeare's *Twelfth Night* in 1941, presented by the Chekhov Theatre Players, in addition to demonstrations of his acting technique and productions of plays at the Chekhov Theatre Studio in Ridgefield, Connecticut.

Michael Chekhov, for his part, welcomed the challenge of working with young Broadway actors faced with a competitive commercial theatre, actors who wanted to understand more deeply the finer aspects of their craft, in the firm belief that doing so would help to create a new kind of theatre.

At this point in his career, Chekhov had an established studio and a theatre in Ridgefield, a studio in New York, and a company of actors, trained in his method, who were becoming seasoned members of a traveling theatrical troupe. The Chekhov Theatre Players had already completed two tours through the eastern and southern parts of the country, and had just embarked on a third tour which would take them as far away as the Texas Panhandle and the Middle West. Their repertoire included *King Lear, Twelfth Night,* an adaptation of *The Cricket on the Hearth,* and *Troublemaker-Doublemaker,* an original play for children by Chekhov himself, in collaboration with Arnold Sundgaard. For Chekhov, the touring company was more than a successful artistic and financial venture. It was the fulfillment of a vision and promise made when the Chekhov Theatre Studio was established at Dartington Hall in England in 1935: to form a touring company of studio actors after three years of training. By the quality of its acting and productions, the company would carry to a wide audience Chekhov's ideas and principles for the theatre of the future, in which he so passionately believed. It would be a new kind of theatre, with a new kind of actor, an actor trained and skilled in every aspect of the theatre —an actor in love with his profession, the embodiment of all that Chekhov taught. This vision had been achieved.

When the group of professional New York actors approached Chekhov with the suggestion that he give them an introductory course in his method, he was enjoying a breathing spell, devoting time to writing his book, and preparing another Shakespeare production for the touring company. He believed there was an audience out there longing for such plays. After the departure of the touring company, despite war clouds gathering on the horizon, Chekhov was free to work with the actors.

A series of fourteen classes was held in the New York Studio. Chekhov introduced the principles of his method to the actor-students through a vigorous period of training in psycho-physical exercises, aimed at freeing the actor's body and emotions. These were followed by improvisations, and finally by scenes from plays. All of this material, vividly presented by Chekhov, was directed at arousing the actor's nature. There was an element of performance, of continuous inner acting on his part, which was dramatic and exciting for the students. Although he seldom demonstrated a point, preferring that the students discover it for themselves, they felt the varied colors and nuances which wove through his teaching, fascinating and inspiring their imaginations by his fire.

The device of "Questions and Answers" which Chekhov used in his classes with the professional actors proved to be both stimulating and provocative, keeping them concentrated and challenged while Chekhov's highly original approach to theatre problems was given full sway. Many of the exercises were accompanied by music, played by a pianist-composer, introducing the elements of rhythm, movement, and gesture which fascinated Chekhov, and were crucial to his method.

As Chekhov's assistant, I kept a record of all class work by means of shorthand notes. In the transcribed material comprising this collection, a vivid picture emerges of a highly gifted theatre artist, moving among his actor-students, presenting always fresh and original aspects of the theatre.

In person, Michael Chekhov was slight, and moved with a lightness and ease, the personification of "the feeling of ease" and "weightlessness" which he encouraged in his students. These qualities were quickly transferred to them, so that in a very short time their often cumbersome bodies began to respond and to become transformed, thus releasing the actor's feeling nature which had been blocked by his inarticulate physical form. This, for Chekhov, was always the beginning basic training for old or young, trained or beginning actor: the throwing off of physical constraints, permitting the feelings and emotions to be expressed through the actor's instrument, his new-found flexible and responsive body.

Chekhov had acquired an amazing facility in his use of the English language, enabling him to impart his original, imaginative suggestions to his students. This had not always been so. I remember the first lesson he gave to Beatrice Straight and me in New York in 1935. There he stood, an elegant figure with black fedora hat and walking stick, smiling and ready to begin teaching, but without one word of English at his command except "How do you do?" delivered with a slight bow. Mme. Tamara Daykarhanova acted as interpreter, while I took notes in shorthand of these very first classes, never dreaming how many more were to follow. Scarcely more than a year later, Chekhov stood before his first class of twenty students at the Chekhov Theatre Studio at Dartington Hall, and with facility, clarity, and grace gave a lesson on "The Future Culture and the Importance of Technique." He was alluding to a brilliant display of technique in a performance by Uday Shankar and his Hindu Ballet, given to celebrate the opening of the Studio, which had aroused his deep admiration as well as providing an object lesson for his new students.

Michael Chekhov was a warm, compassionate human being. He loved his profession, which he considered to be of a spiritual nature. He loved his actors and his students, and spent his life on their behalf exploring new ways in which to free the body, voice and imagination of the actor-artist, and to establish in him confidence in his power to enter into and live in the world of the creative imagination. Paramount for Chekhov was the search for ever deeper and more creative powers. He could be demanding and stern, but only as a means of bringing out the best in his students. A lesson with him was always a revelation. The realm of the creative imagination was Chekhov's home throughout his artistic life, although the practical business aspects of the theatre also had their own validity and were worthy of his closest attention.

Chekhov drew on that great stream of knowledge, gained through the sound training he had received in the Moscow Art Theatre and its First Studio under Stanislavsky, who was his mentor and friend, and later through his association with Max Reinhardt in Berlin and Vienna, and with other outstanding European companies and artists. His ideas and ideals were forged into what later became his method. Always striving, always searching, he had the courage to discard whatever had outgrown its usefulness and to replace it with fresh insights, so that his method never became dull or didactic, thus providing a relief from the prevalent overly-analytical approach to the theatre. Reinhardt is quoted as saying, "Michael Chekhov is a genius," and Stanislavsky, in evaluating the young Chekhov for his work in the First Studio, wrote: "Talent very fascinating. One of our hopes for the future." Today in Russia, where Chekhov has been rehabilitated after more than fifty years as a "non-person," he is referred to as "the acting genius of the century."

No one who has worked with Michael Chekhov will ever forget the experience. In the sense of warmth and assurance which flowed from him to his students, as he stepped into the classroom to begin his transformation work with them, he embodied the crossing of the threshold, the feeling of ease, beauty, form and the whole, the center, the archetype, the psychological gesture, the imaginary body, the pause, atmosphere, contact, continuous acting, radiation, inspiration and all the other beautiful, subtle points of his method, as revealed in *Lessons for the Professional Actor*.

Deirdre Hurst du Prey

December 1984
Westbury, N.Y.

Introduction

Mel Gordon

The teaching of acting outside the theatre, unrelated to any specific production or troupe, is a twentieth-century anomaly. Except for the dozen or so
"greats," working in a "secret" or intuitive fashion, one became a professional
actor by copying other already successful performers. To learn his craft, as with
any other trade, a student-actor apprenticed with older actors. It would be difficult to identify more than a handful of schools that exclusively taught theatre
practicum before 1890 in Europe. And even these miniature academies were
hardly better than glorified sessions in stage diction and deportment—really,
finishing schools with a bit of aesthetic pretension for the children of the
wealthy. Despite valiant attempts by nineteenth-century reformers like Fran-
çois Delsarte, William Macready, Steele MacKaye, and Richard Mansfield, they
provided only scenic fodder for the reigning stars of the day and their dramatic
vehicles.

The growing acceptance of new kinds of theatre at the turn-of-the-century,
with its thirst for novelty especially in styles of acting, however, changed all
this. Suddenly, there was a need for innovative methodologies in training. To
understand Michael Chekhov and the unique qualities of his 1941 classes, it is
useful first to look at his own background and schooling with Konstantin
Stanislavsky during this pioneer period of actor and teacher interaction.

When he should have been flushed with the directorial triumph of his
Moscow Art Theatre's German tour in 1905, Stanislavsky found himself in a
morass of depression. He knew what he wanted in his actors and in himself,
but did not know how to achieve it. A scientific system of actor preparation
was needed. What had taken him decades to learn about performance through
the traditional means of observation and imitation, scholarly research, and hit-

or-miss onstage experience could be systemized and taught, Stanislavsky felt. Even famous actors wasted years and years learning the basic principles of their calling, frequently in an undisciplined and amateurish environment. To counter this, to transform the simplistic notion of acting as a bohemian and erratic vocation into one of deep and creative artistry, Stanislavsky formed a new school and workshop, the First Studio, an experimental unit of the established Moscow Art Theatre. And it was here at the First Studio, where Chekhov trained, that a contemporary analysis of the nature of acting and actor education took root.

If the MAT and the First Studio were powerful magnets for the great young theatrical talents of pre-revolutionary Russia—out of tens of hundreds of serious candidates, only a handful were accepted each year—they also created their own internal effusion and unraveling. Both, Vladimir Nemirovich-Danchenko, the MAT's co-founder, and Vsevolod Meyerhold, a promising young actor and director in 1905, evolved from Stanislavsky's most celebrated devotees to embittered rebels. And later the pioneering talents of the First Studio—persons like Leopold Sulzerzhitky, the custodian of the MAT, suddenly made head of the Studio; Evgeni Vakhtangov, Michael Chekhov, and even Richard Boleslavsky—found themselves often moving far beyond the aesthetic pale of their teacher's theories. The relationships between Stanislavsky and his most able disciples all seemed to follow a peculiar pattern: an initial period of personal loyalty and blind acceptance of the work; a stormy blow-up during the rehearsal of major production over some feature of the System; expulsion from Stanislavsky's inner circle; a personal reconciliation brought about by the master himself during a super-dramatic crisis (e.g., the slow deaths of Sulzer and Vakhtangov); and finally Stanislavsky's incorporation of his critics' innovations some ten or fifteen years after they were first suggested.

Michael Chekhov's personal relationship with Stanislavsky moved along the same bumpy road as his classmates did although with even more mad complicity and intensity. For one thing, Chekhov lived longer than the other rebels and his basic disagreements with Stanislavsky were more theatrically extreme. So extreme, in fact, that few followers of either Chekhov or Stanislavsky have seen much positive connection between their respective theories or practices in actor-training. The actual classroom transcriptions of Stanislavsky and Chekhov, however, reveal stronger and more complimentary links than their "official" textbooks might suggest.

Born into a middle-class St. Petersburg family in 1891, Michael Chekhov was marked for his entire life as "the nephew of Chekhov" (the playwright, Anton Chekhov). While this "halo/stigmata" helped Michael in times of obscurity, especially at the beginning of his Russian career and during the wandering years of exile in the West, its overall effect was psychologically debilitating. Although Chekhov often worried about accusations of nepotism or allowing himself to be used like a side-show curiosity, the simple taking of another

name—as, for instance, Stanislavsky had—seems to have never seriously oc-
cured to him. Like other difficulties in his career, Chekhov saw this as a sym-
bolic obstacle to be accepted and transformed into an artistic expression, rather
than an objective problem to be overcome or avoided.

A young character actor at the Maly Theatre, Chekhov was invited by
Stanislavsky in 1909 to join the MAT. Trained by Vakhtangov, Stanislavsky's
star pupil, Chekhov appeared as walk-ons in various MAT productions, including the Gordon Craig *Hamlet*. During a performance of *The Imaginary In-
valid*, Stanislavsky reprimanded young Chekhov for "having too much fun
with the part." While professing perfect belief in Stanislavsky's System of acting, Chekhov found himself in trouble from the very beginning.

Cast by Boleslavsky in the First Studio's "test" production, *The Wreck of the
"Good Hope"* in 1913, Chekhov created quite a stir. He took the minor role of
Kobe, the idiot fisherman, and metamorphosized him into a creature of pathos
and intense lyricism, altering the character, through movement and make-up,
from a low-comedy type into a sincere and morbid seeker of truth. When
criticized that his notion of Kobe was not what Herman Heyermans, the Dutch
playwright, intended, Chekhov replied that he went beyond the playwright
and the play to find Kobe's true character.

The idea that an actor can "go beyond the playwright or the play" is the first
key in understanding the Chekhov Method and how it differed from Stanislavsky's early teachings. In his 1928 autobiography, Chekhov wrote about a pre-
MAT revelation that shaped his novel thinking on characterization: "The
masterly productions of B.S. Glagolin produced an ineradicable impression on
me. When I saw him in the part of Khlestakov [from Nikolai Gogol's *Inspector
General* in a 1910 Maly production], I underwent a kind of mental shift. It
became clear to me that Glagolin plays the part of Khlestakov *not like others*,
although I had never before seen anyone else in that part. And this feeling 'not
like others' arose in me." In other words, Chekhov, like Stanislavsky, was in
search of new conceptual models onto which he could "hang" his characters,
moving away from imitations of commercial actors and other, expected stage
clichés. Whereas Stanislavsky found the "truth" of his stage personalities in
enactments based on real human behavior, Chekhov sought a stronger, more
fantastic depth of feeling through the play of his imagination and intuition.

There is no doubt that Stanislavsky and others appreciated Chekhov's
finished products—Stanislavsky had long pronounced Chekhov "his most
brilliant pupil," and Chekhov's Russian fans ran into the tens of thousands
before and after the Revolution. What concerned the MAT crowd was
Chekhov's erratic means of creating character. One semi-apocryphal story may
explain their theatrical conflict. Asked by Stanislavsky to enact a true dramatic
situation as an exercise in emotional memory, Chekhov recreated his wistful
presence at his father's funeral. Overwhelmed by its novel detail and sense of
truth, Stanislavsky embraced Michael, thinking that this was yet another proof

of the power of real affective memory for the actor. Unfortunately, Stanislav-sky later found out that Chekhov's ailing father was, in fact, still alive and Chekhov's performance was based on a feverish anticipation of the event. Reprimanded once again, Chekhov was dropped from the class due "to an over-heated imagination."

Between 1913 and 1923, Chekhov appeared in twelve MAT and indepen-dent productions, usually as a lead or in important supporting roles. His reputation as an actor and as later an independent thinker in the theatre in-creased dramatically despite bouts of depression brought about by the deaths of family members, war hysteria, revolution, and alcoholism. The first two years after the Bolshevik victory, 1918 and 1919, were especially crucial to Chekhov's spiritual and artistic growth. Unable to continue performing the part of Malvolio—enacted in the typical Chekhov style of sharply felt contrasts: here, of sweet, lyrical sensibilities embedded in a "swamp" of grotesque eroticism—at the First Studio's *Twelfth Night*, Chekhov was reduced to a "gaunt brooding soul, weighed down by Russia's sorrows," according to the visiting American critic, Oliver Sayler. Within months, Chekhov developed an acute paranoia, believing that he could hear and "see" faraway conversations. Thoughts of suicide and his mother's death interrupted his every activity. By the Spring of 1918, Chekhov's immediate family life deteriorated. His wife Olga divorced him, taking their newborn daughter. Stanislavsky had a team of psychiatrists diagnose his troublesome, but still favorite, actor. Finally, Chekhov underwent a series of hypnotic treatments. All this brought an end to the worst of Chekhov's psychological espisodes, but he was still subject to fits of uncon-trollable laughter.

More than the advanced therapies or cures of Stanislavsky's physicians, it was the discovery of Hindu philosophy and, sometime after that, of Rudolf Steiner's Anthroposophy that altered Chekhov's psychic condition. In fact, Chekhov's passionate investigation of Steiner's spiritual science filled a dangerous chasm in Chekhov's creative world as it unblocked a choking emo-tional life. Suddenly, Chekhov understood his maddening lack of will was the residue of a spiritual crisis rather than the chemical unbalance of an overwork-ed actor. Chekhov began to reason that his strangely timed breakdown—at the height of his career—was actually his soul's silent protest against what he was becoming as a performer: a malevolent vessel of drunken egotism. In many ways, Chekhov in 1919 resembled the Stanislavsky of 1905, "praised but unhappy"; both longed for a more perfect system of actor-training, but Chekhov also sought a more perfect style of acting—one that contained a larger and deeper component, more akin to the joyous religiosity of the classical Greeks than the petty commercialism and politics of Chekhov's Russia.

The Anthroposophists' demonstrations of Speech-Formation (a kind of vocal symbolization) and the modern dance-like Eurhythmy (called "the science of visible speech" (made a great impression on Chekhov. Like the mantras and various yogas of Hinduism and Buddhism, Steiner's physical disciplines provided a sophisticated and clearly-delineated outlet for his pupils. In addition, performances that utilized Eurhythmy—either as dance or in Steiner's Mystery-Dramas—attracted a wide audience following at Anthroposophical centers in Germany and Switzerland. Although Chekhov did not meet with Steiner until 1922 during a Central European tour, his contacts with local Russian Anthroposophical groups were frequent and productive. More important, they simulated Chekhov's ideas for a future or perfect theatre.

Marrying the inner truth and emotional depth of Stanislavsky's system with the beauty and spiritual impact of Steiner's work became Chekhov's obsession. In 1920, he opened his own studio in the Arbat district of Moscow. It was the first of several such attempts to pass on his singular form of acting. But, as always, financial considerations forced him back on the stage. Early in 1921, Chekhov starred in Vakhtangov's gloomy, proto-Expressionist *Erik IV* by Strindberg. Playing a young but impotent King in a corrupt court, Chekhov discovered the character's nature by internalizing a handful of startling images. Inspired by the lessons of Eurhythmy, Chekhov "found" his role by experimenting with the shape and quality of the character's movement and rearrangements of his body size. Only when he "saw" the character, could Chekhov begin his embodiment, or incorporation, of the role. Simultaneous with *Erik XIV*, Chekhov was in rehearsal for *The Inspector General*, under Stanislavsky's direction. His interpretation of Khlestakov was so unusual and his embodiment physically so different from Chekhov's normal look that a shocked Vakhtangov whispered to Stanislavsky on opening night, "Can this be the same man we see in the Studio every morning?" Again the notion of "not like others."

By 1924, after Vakhtangov's death and the MAT's celebrated tour of Western Europe and America, Stanislavsky rewarded Chekhov with the directorship of his own theatre, the Second Moscow Art Theatre. Freed of other worries, Chekhov began to experiment in earnest. Exercises in rhythmic movement and telepathic communication filled the members' crowded schedules. In preparation for a controversial *Hamlet*, Chekhov taught his actors to use Shakespeare's language like a physical property, tossing balls as they rehearsed their lines. Neither the actor's personality nor stage clichés of the director or playwight were allowed to be the basis of any role. Chekhov spoke of finding the archetype, or the "correct" image, of the character—much like Plato's shadows that patiently wait to be discovered. Although he appeared more of a leading actor than artistic director, Chekhov's approach soon became subject to severe criticism. Denounced as an "idealist" and mystic in 1927, Alexei Diky and sixteen performers left the Second MAT. Immediately following the split, the foremost Moscow newspapers branded Chekhov as "a sick artist"; his productions "alien and reactionary."

Invited by Max Reinhardt to Berlin to perform the next spring, Chekhov started a second phase of his career, a series of "wander years" in volunteer exile across Central, Western, and Eastern Europe. For seven years—most of them filled with disappointments—Chekhov pursued his life-long quest to create his own troupe and method of actor-training. In Austria and in Berlin, Chekhov starred in German-language comedies and silent films. After months of negotiation in 1931, he organized a Russian-language theatre in Paris, but its financial backing never fully materialized. Finally with the help of Georgette Boner, a young pupil of Reinhardt, Chekhov set up studios in Paris and one year later in the independent republics of Latvia and Lithuania. But the threat of war and fascist coup in the Baltics sent Chekhov temporarily back to Western Europe and then, by the invitation of Sol Hurok, to America.

Opening on Broadway in the Spring of 1935 as the head of the "Moscow Art Players," Chekhov accomplished two difficult tasks: he took the theatre intelligentsia by storm with his Russian-language productions, and he found at long last a sensitive and talented benefactor, Beatrice Straight. With her companion, Deirdre Hurst (soon to be Chekhov's secretary), Straight brought Chekhov to Dartington Hall, the site of her family estate in Devonshire, England. Amidst other experimental projects in agriculture and small-craft industry, Chekhov set the foundations of a new theatre. There, in Dartington's utopian community created in 1925 by Straight's step-father and mother, Leonard and Dorothy Elmhirst, the trio of Hurst, Straight, and Chekhov recruited instructors and students for the study of the Chekhov Method. Drawn from the United States, England, Canada, Australia, New Zealand, Germany, Austria, Norway, and Lithuania, two dozen young actors were to become the initiates of Chekhov's twenty-five-year-old dream.

Atmospheres, the Awakening Exercises, Centering, Incorporation, Psychological Gesture, Radiation—nearly the entire pantheon of Chekhov's Method was set at Dartington. Although adjustments and changes were made later at Ridgefield, Connecticut and in New York and Hollywood, Chekhov's essential format had been articulated by 1937-38, Dartington's second term. The training there was thorough and deliberate, lasting two full years. It was also a time of good feelings among the faculty and pupils, punctuated with high and intense artistic aspirations. But British expectations of war with Germany in 1939 caused the Chekhov Theatre Studio to relocate across the Atlantic in rural Connecticut.

The Ridgefield Studio physically resembled Dartington in certain ways, yet its proximity to New York City changed Chekhov's way of thinking about his school and instruction. First of all, Chekhov allowed himself to be persuaded by George Shadanoff, a friend and director, to mount a large Broadway production—the unsuccessful The Possessed, adapted from Dostoyevsky's masterpiece. Secondly, Chekhov began to think about the development of classes for working, experienced actors. Despite three highly-praised and hugely ambitious Chekhov Theatre Studio tours outside New York City in New England, the midwest, and the deep south between 1940 and 1942, the single Broadway fiasco and other difficulties at Ridgefield weighed heavily on Chekhov's mind.

In the Fall of 1941, the Chekhov Theatre opened a New York studio on 56th Street. The Manhattan move brought Chekhov to a critical point in his long and unpredictable career. It had been over a decade since the Moscow and Berlin theatre reviewers bestowed their accolades on him, and Chekhov's fame as a Hollywood character actor and teacher was still four or five years in the future. In addition to classes in the Chekhov Method (conducted by Chekhov, George Shadanoff, Alan Harkness, Beatrice Straight, and Deirdre Hurst), a full curriculum of Speech Training (Steiner's Speech-Formation led by Ann Veith Greenley), Eurhythmy (Ruth Pusch), Music Appreciation, Choral Singing, Fencing, Gymnastics (H. L. Pusch), and Makeup was offered. The twice-weekly two-hour classes for professional actors, however, were of special importance for Chekhov. Here Chekhov hoped to perfect and summarize all of the features of his technique.

That members and associates of the recently disbanded Group Theatre filled Chekhov's professional class should have been of little surprise. After all, it was among the Group Theatre actors in 1935 that Chekhov made his largest impact. Stella Adler, Morris Carnovsky, Bobby Lewis, Sandy Meisner, and others borrowed basic scenic ideas and exercises from Chekhov's demonstrations and workshops. Chekhov also acted as a cipher for much of the Group, symbolizing a kind of imaginative training totally alien from Lee Strasberg's interpretations of Stanislavsky and Vakhtangov. Indirectly, Chekhov provided the strongest intellectual counterweight to Strasberg's much criticized Method.

Although the differences between the various techniques of Stanislavsky, Chekhov, and Strasberg were and are distinct, a strong vein of agreement runs through all of them: to produce a fresh form of acting that contains a piercing emotional depth and sense of truth. As Stanislavsky wrote, a talented performer who utilizes his System may not look any better on the stage than a similarly talented, untrained actor, but the truthful effects created by the Stanislavsky actor will be remembered by audiences far longer. To a large degree, the variations between the three methods are not unnecessarily in scenic outcome (for instance, each teacher loved Kabuki), but in language and process.

Chekhov attempted to use a vocabulary that spoke directly to the performer's mind and imagination. Most directors and coaches, including Stanislavsky and Strasberg, tell the actor what they want in abstract terms. This causes the performer to reinterpret each command according to the workings of his brain and musculature. The instruction to relax, for example, a frequent directorial request, often produces a number of secondary responses in the actor's mind: "Although I feel relaxed, some part of my body is tense. First I must figure where; I'll start with my shoulders. . . ." The Chekhov Method deals primarily with images, especially visceral ones that short circuit most self-conscious reactions. Instead of telling the actor to relax, Chekhov asked him, "To walk (or to sit or stand) with a feeling of ease." Rather than demand a slouching performer, playing a proud aristocrat, "To sit up straight," Chekhov told him to let his body "think 'up.'" While the dissimilarities between Chekhov's linguistic approach and the others may seem petty to the non-actor, for Chekhov and his followers, they were crucial, for it signalled a profound technical understanding of the actor's intellect and consciousness.

Many of Chekhov's exercises fell into certain distinct categories. Some had a lightness and even "party" feel to them. For the most part, this was intentional. In order to open up "new" areas of mind, Chekhov made actor-training fun. The internal censors that prevent many actors from attempting untried ideas and roles—"not to appear stupid or ridiculous"—cease to function normally when the work is framed in a non-adult, or risk-free, manner. Chekhov also created blocks of exercises that produced a rush of exhilaration or energy in his students. For Chekhov, the loss of mental energy or enthusiasm was one of the greatest obstacles to the creation of character, "the sense of aliveness on stage."

More than anything else, Chekhov's work became associated with the use of imagination. Since the theatre's power is in its ability to communicate through imagery, rather than in literary concepts, Chekhov sought to uncover the appropriate actor-training devices. His improvisations advanced the notion that scenic space could have a special, almost magical, character filled with combustible or intoxicating atmospheres. Where Strasberg's emotional memory exercises played upon the actor's sensory recall of an actual event, which then had to be used as a substitute in a similar occurence in a script, Chekhov schooled his students in finding imaginary, external stimuli to fire their emotions. Chekhov believed, for instance, one had only to visualize and viscerally experience the presence of a huge Gothic cathedral to feel true awe or amazement. Always known for his detailed and unusual dramatic interpretations, Chekhov gave particular attention at the Studio to the creation of character, too. Normally a missing link in modern acting techniques, characterization was broken down by Chekhov into precise steps: finding the character's center; imaging his body; discovering his Psychological Gesture, etc.

The 1941 transcriptions for this book made by Deirdre Hurst du Prey give the reader one of the fullest accounts of Chekhov as a teacher and actor. Unlike Chekhov's *To the Actor*, published in 1953, or the 1963 *To the Director and Playwright*, which has been curiously "compiled and written by Charles Leonard," *Lessons for the Professional Actor* reveal Chekhov in his most natural and vivacious state: before live performers in a theatre-like environment. Only slightly edited from du Prey's original notes, Chekhov's words reach out to us, his "Future Actors," and capture those restless areas of our mind that need to make art. Chekhov accomplishes this effortlessly, using his two best weapons: truth and imagination.

LIST OF PARTICIPANTS

Jack Arnold	Nov-Jan 42	[Broadway]
John Berry	Nov-Jan 42	
Phoebe Brand	Nov-Feb 42	[Group Theatre]
Phil Brown	Nov-Jan 42	
Donald Buka	Nov-Jan 42	[Broadway]
Rosalind Carter	Nov-Feb 42	[Broadway]
Morris Carnovsky	Nov-Dec 41	[Group Theatre]
Bert Conway	Nov-Jan 42	[Group Theatre]
Curt Conway	Nov-Feb 42	[Group Theatre]
Phil Conway	Nov-Jan 42	[Group Theatre]
Oliva Deering	Nov-Dec 41	[Federal Theatre]
Rosalind Fradkin	Dec-Mar 42	[Vassar Theatre]
Arthur Franz	Dec-Mar 42	[Broadway]
Peter Frye	Nov-Jan 42	[Group Theatre]
Fred Herrick	Dec-Feb 42	[Broadway]
Mary Hunter	Nov-Jan 42	[Americn Actors Co.]
Leon Janney	Nov-Jan 42	[Radio]
Timothy Kearse	Nov-Mar 42	[Broadway]
Marian Kopp	Nov-Jan 42	
Catheryn Laughlin	Nov-Dec 41	[Group Theatre]
Elenor Lynn	Nov-Jan 42	[Group Theatre]
Anna Minot	Dec-Feb/Jun 42	
Martha Picken	Nov-Mar 42	[Broadway]
Martin Ritt	Feb/Jun 42	[Group Theatre]
Alfred Ryder	Nov-Jan 42	[Group Theatre]
Michael Strong	Nov-Jan 42	[Broadway]
Paula Strasberg	Nov-Dec 41	[Group Theatre]
Shea Thelma	Nov-Jan 42	[Broadway]
Tamara	Nov-Jan 42	[Group Theatre]
Perry Wilson	Nov-Jan 42	
Lynn Whitney	Nov-Jan 42	
Elizabeth Zemach	Nov-Jan 42	

First Class

Why is a Method Needed in the Theatre of Today?

November 7, 1941

THE NEED FOR AN ACTING TECHNIQUE

I think today will be a kind of introduction as I will speak mainly in general. First of all, let us ask why is a method needed in the theatre? It seems that the theatre goes on so well without any such difficulties as a "method." Yes, it can go on like that and will go on for a long time, but still it seems to me that the time will come when every one of us will become somehow unhappy, simply because our profession lacks a technique—excuse me if I say things that offend you about our profession, but I must speak honestly to you what I feel about the theatre, and perhaps you will forgive me when you realize that I also am an actor and, therefore, offend myself in offending you.

Sometime we will realize that our profession is the only one which has no technique. A painter has to develop a technique, a musician, a dancer, every artist, but somehow we actors are left alone—we are acting because we want to act, and we act just as it goes. Something must be wrong.

This painful feeling that our profession has no technique made me unhappy to the extent that I tried to find what kind of technique it could be. And then I saw that our profession is even more difficult than any other, because we have only one instrument to convey to the audience our feelings, our emotions, our ideas—our own body. It is terrifyingly true.

THE ACTOR'S BODY AS AN INSTRUMENT

I use this same body for everything in my daily life, I use my voice for everything, for quarreling, for making love, for expressing my indifference. It is strange to realize that I have nothing more to show to the audience than myself. I found it difficult to find a justification for using the most abused thing in my life, my body, as something which I have to show every evening as a new thing, interesting, attractive. My own body, my own emotions, my own voice . . . I have nothing except myself.

Then I understood that if it is so that the actor cannot have a musical instrument or a brush, or paint, then he must have a special kind of technique which he must find inside himself. If we find this technique, or at least the approach to this hidden, mysterious thing sitting in ourselves, then maybe we shall get to the point where we shall hope to have a technique.

After many years of trying to find this technique I found that everything we need in order to develop such a technique is already there in us, if we are born as actors. That means that we have only to find out which sides of our own nature have to be stressed, underlined, exercised, and the whole technique will be there. Because while we act, good or bad, we are using our own nature but in a very chaotic way, in such a way that one part of our nature is disturbing the other part and the third part comes in between, and something else falls down upon us, etc. But the elements are there, the thing is how to anatomize our own nature—to find what is a, b, c, and d, and then when "a" is well-shaped and "b" is well-shaped, we can let these letters come intuitively together and create words which will mean something and will not be so chaotic.

I have found three things—when I say "found," I mean I have been attentive to certain points and they have become obvious; I have invented nothing—the three realms which have, first of all, to be distinguished: 1) our bodies 2) our voices 3) our emotions. At first I thought that we must keep each one of them apart and try to develop them as if in different rooms. But I found that when we start to develop the body, for instance, we find a very interesting thing. Trying to make exercises with our bodies only, in a purely physical way, we find gradually that we are already in the other room where our emotions are. So that our body becomes, later on, nothing other than our psychology incorporated in our whole body—hands, fingers, eyes, etc.

THE ACTOR'S PSYCHOLOGY

Thus, the body becomes part of our psychology, which is a very interesting experience and a very surprising one. Suddenly we feel that this same body which we use the whole day through for going here and there, this body is a different one when we are on the stage, because there it becomes, as it were, my condensed, crystallized psychology. If I have something inside me, it becomes my hand, my arm, my cheek, my eye, etc.

Then we go into the other room, where pure psychology is—nothing to do with the body, only ideas, feelings, will, impulse, etc.,—and we try to develop them as purely psychological things. Suddenly we discover that it is our body also. If I am unhappy, it is my body, my face, my arms, my hands, every part of me becomes unhappy if I have trained my body sufficiently, but it is possible only if my psychology has been developed separately from the beginning.

THE INTELLECT

Then they, the body and the psychology, find each other somewhere in the subconscious regions of our creative soul, and when they meet each other, we find the following thing: that all that we have to do on the stage is to find out gradually that when the developed psychology and the developed body find each other and join together in our subconscious life, then we have to exclude one disturbing element in our profession. It is our dry intellect which tries to interfere with our emotions, with our body, with our art. Intellect in the sense of dry thinking. Perhaps you will help me find the right term because actually "intellect" is a very high term. But by intellect, we mean a cold, dry, analytical approach to things which cannot be approached in this way. This is the only difficulty we must exclude.

We have to rely on the training of our bodies on the one hand, and the training of our emotions on the other, and on excluding this intellect for the time being. This does not mean that one has to become a fool—but to rely upon our emotions, on our bodies, and not to rely upon this clear, cold thinking, this "murderer," which sits in our head. Later on it will become very useful when it sees that it cannot kill the body or the emotions, because it is in the actor's power. I can become gay and laugh, or sorry and thoughtful as I wish because I have trained myself.

Then the intellect becomes very useful because it makes clear for me everything in my profession—starting with the written play and finishing with the production on the stage. Every detail becomes full of meaning, full of sense, because the intellect knows that it cannot do anything but serve me. But to start by making agreements with the intellect, to fawn before it, to obey it, then we are lost. When the intellect is allowed to become the master, it becomes a fool, an evil fool and a merciless one. Everything which the intellect can make clear it makes obscure if it knows, "I am the only master." Then we are lost.

THE ACTOR'S VOICE

So the first scheme I want to convey to you is to anatomize the body, emotions, and voice and have nothing to do with the intellect. The body becomes the soul and the soul the body, and the intellect is allowed to come and serve. The voice is a special thing and a very interesting one. I cannot speak about the voice here because it is not my special field, but the method which we use in our school, that of Dr. Rudolf Steiner, is a very interesting and profound one, and also the results are not immediately obvious, and this is very good. When the results are there, they are of such a kind that our voice becomes a fine instrument for expressing and conveying the most subtle psychological things. The technique of using our voice according to this method is of such kind that we can send the voice either in high or low tones over a distance which seems sometimes impossible.

THE ORIGINS OF THE THEATRE

The second point is—speaking again only in general—that very often we professional people forget one thing. We forget that everything which starts must be finished—just as with a plant. The seed is put into the ground, the long process of growing takes place, and another seed is the result and goes into the ground again, etc., etc. Just so with the theatre. Once the human race found it necessary to express and experience for itself certain things which they called "theatre." You know, of course, the origin of the theatre and how profound and deep it is. After this profound experience which humanity had—mostly religious, many thousands of years ago—the process of using the theatre degenerated more and more and went to the most ignoble depths. But the beginning was very high and the end will be still higher.

Therefore, there is very much to do in the theatre. Many things have to be rediscovered so that the beginning will become the end. And I think we must do everything we can to make the theatre more noble, more complicated, as it were, because this will serve our human culture more than anything else. All the moral preaching is nothing in comparison with the theatre, if one has the vision as to what will be the end of this beginning. And if one has only the courage to say that we are in a state of degeneration.

THE DEGENERATION OF THE THEATRE

What was at the beginning, and what must be at the end, and what is the degeneration? In the beginning, as you know, the theatre was the means of getting certain impulses from somewhere else to enrich one's experience. The end will be to enrich the surrounding life by giving back all the experiences which the human being can accumulate more and more, and become so rich and full of precious ideas, emotions, and will impulses and give them back through the theatre. The moment of degeneration is the little, dry, condensed, egotistical self—I am a very small little thing, and I am showing on the stage how I love, how I hate—me, me, me. This is degeneration, this condensed and closed, "I Am," is the sign that the theatre has degenerated, and instead of getting things, or giving things, one enjoys oneself on the stage in the most egotistical and selfish way.

THE ACTOR'S RELATIONSHIP
TO THE CONTEMPORARY LIFE

The whole life which we have now can be used again for accumulating things, and for preserving them in our souls, if we want to be actors who are inclined to go this way. For instance, to say to oneself, there is a war. Of course, we cannot really imagine what is going on over there, or we would become insane. This lack of imagination allows us to go on living—but to a certain extent we can, we are obliged to imagine the war there. We are obliged to live, for instance, with our dreams. We awaken in the morning, and we know we have dreamed, but we don't think any more about it. But we must make an effort sometimes to remember our dreams upon awakening—why we were laughing or crying, happy, sad, etc. Or I have to imagine the psychology of Hitler, for instance, although it is a very unpleasant business. To penetrate into this man—the most unimaginative mind in the world because he does not know what he is doing, therefore, he has no imagination—only a will and nothing more. But we have to understand what he is, or we have nothing to do on the stage. Just as we have to understand Francis of Assisi as much as we can. We will not become insane if we do this consciously, and by our own will. We will remain absolutely sane, but if *we* deny this necessity to penetrate into these minds *they* will penetrate into ours, and then we will become insane.

This moment will come, but it is better that we do it ourselves and enrich our actor's soul. Then, if we have found some slight understanding of Francis of Assisi and Hitler, and all that lies between them, then it may happen that we appear before the audience on the stage, and suddenly we will be able to produce such things, have such radiation, that Francis of Assisi will act there, so will Hitler, but they will be used and will serve us because we have understood and digested them.

THE THEATRE OF THE FUTURE

These are the means which I believe we, as contemporary actors, must use in order to come out of this state of degeneration; consciously to absorb things and let them live in us and torture us—we have to suffer if we have anything to say, because if we are only happy, we have nothing to say. Then, when we have Francis of Assisi and Hitler in us somewhere, we will inevitably realize what the theatre can and will be some day.

We shall understand many things. First of all, we will see that all the points in our Method are keys which open our own nature for us. All those closed doors, behind which we shall find Hitler whom we manage and govern, and Francis of Assisi who inspires us. All the black things we possess, all the white things we get, and then we can mix the colors and they will mix themselves inside us. Then we shall really enjoy our profession because we have the vision of the future theatre. We have our own actor's creative nature in our own will, and, as actors and artists, we have more than we have as private persons. As private persons, we "know" very little but these little things are so big they make up the whole life for us. This is point two. We will make all these points more concrete by taking each point of the Method separately.

THE PERFORMANCE

We will not make a great mistake if we compare the performance as an independent being, with the individual human being. We know that human beings have ideas, thoughts, and that we have our feelings and emotions, which are quite different from what we call thought or ideas, and we also have our will impulses. Three different regions which can be separated one from the other— 1) ideas 2) feelings 3) will impulses.

The same is true of the performance—I don't mean the written play because that is only the score, only the symbol and indication of what we have to add, but it is not yet the performance. I mean the performance on the stage where everything lives, moves and exists.

THE ATMOSPHERE

The performances as an independent being has also the idea, the "what" that is going to be shown. All that we have on the stage which is "what," is the world of ideas on the stage. Then we have in the performance the realm of feelings, the heart-beat, as it were, and these we call the "atmosphere" of the performance. It is not the feelings of this or that actor, it is the feeling which belongs to the performance itself, to nobody but to the performance.

For instance, let us take some examples to illustrate what I mean by this "atmosphere," which does not belong to anyone but still exists. Let us imagine a street accident—there is a definite atmosphere around the place where the catastrophe has taken place. When you enter the scene where all the people are running or moving or standing still, you, first of all, feel the atmosphere before you understand what it is that has happened. To whom does this "heart-beat" belong? To nobody. The policeman has quite different feelings, but he has not produced the atmosphere. The victim has different feelings, but still it is not the atmosphere of the catastrophe. We look on helplessly, but our mood is also different. To whom does this atmosphere belong?—to no one. You can't find the person who has created this atmosphere of the catastrophe, and still it is there.

This is a very strange thing, and psychologists cannot explain it. They try to figure it out by means of the dry intellect—from where does this atmosphere come and to whom does it belong—it cannot be explained, but it is there. Let us take another example—you enter an old castle. In whatever mood you are in, you feel immediately something of the atmosphere of the castle. Who created this atmosphere? No one is there. The walls, doors, and windows? It is there, and you even feel, just as you did when you underwent the painful atmosphere of the catastrophe on the street, that first there is a little fight between your own mood and feelings and the atmosphere, and either you push it away from you, or you give in to it. Either *it* is stronger than you are, or *you* are stronger than it is. Just the same with the castle—you may enter it in a very gay mood, and suddenly something comes over you. In the castle it is perhaps pleasant to accept the atmosphere and merge with it, but there is still a moment when it is questionable which will conquer—the atmosphere or your will.

Each performance should have an atmosphere which does not belong to anyone but belongs to the performance itself. Each scene in the performance must have its own atmosphere—I say "must" because it is not always there. Why? Because of the intellect we have spoken about, this dry, cold intellect is an enemy not only of our personal feelings, but also of atmospheres in the performance, and of the atmosphere of the performance as a whole, because the intellect cannot stand feelings. It knows that as soon as we allow our heart, as the realm of feelings, to become alive, the intellect immediately feels it has to think differently. All its knowledge and convictions mean nothing at the moment when we allow our heart to produce its values.

THE FEELINGS

In our present culture—not only in America, but in the whole world and before the war, because now it is a bit different—our present disease is that we have closed and shut our hearts to such an extent, that we cannot not only produce atmospheres on the stage, but we are ashamed to show our feelings to each other, knowing that in one's head instinctively sits a devil who will laugh at all our feelings if we dare to show them. If that is so, then, of course, we cannot create any atmosphere on the stage, and we are compelled to show only an imitation of our own personal "I Am" feelings, and "I Am" is not an interesting person—my personal feelings mean nothing when shown from the stage. It has to be something bigger than "I Am." Atmosphere gives us the air, the space around us. It coaxes our deeper feelings and emotions, our dreams, our Francis of Assisi, our Hitler. Without atmosphere we are imprisoned on the stage.

There are certain means by which we can create the atmosphere on the stage and let me tell you in general about them. The atmosphere, "the soul" of the performance, the realm of the feelings, is what our present time needs more than anything else. We are not free inwardly because we are afraid of our own hearts, and the hearts of our fellow actors. First of all, we have to learn, to train ourselves as actors to discover in our everyday life the atmospheres which are around us everywhere. This can be done very consciously. You can enter different rooms, different streets, buildings, etc., and ask yourself what atmosphere is there. Very soon you will see that there are atmospheres everywhere—strongly expressed, powerful atmospheres. This first attempt to understand, to absorb the atmosphere will be the first step to the ability to create it on the stage. For instance, the atmosphere of this room in which we are sitting is a very strong and obvious one. If we pay attention to it, we will realize that it is there and that we have not created it individually.

The second step can be the following. When reading plays, for instance, we can try to find which atmosphere would be the most expressive one for this scene, for this moment, for this part of the scene. We can do this pleasant exercise when reading plays. Take *Othello*, for instance. If you are trained and sensitive to atmosphere, you will find that the tragedy of *Othello* has an atmosphere which you could never confuse with any other of Shakespeare's tragedies. *Twelfth Night* has a definite atmosphere, and so has any modern play. There is nothing in the whole world without atmosphere except our dry, cold intellect which knows nothing about atmosphere and fights it.

The third way to be able to manage atmospheres is to imagine the atmosphere we want to create on the stage, to imagine it objectively as being in the actual air around us. But not yet in us. We can imagine that this room is filled with smoke, with blue smoke, with gray smoke, or with a fragrance. It is easy to imagine that. Or we can imagine that the air is filled with sorrow. It is just as easy as to imagine it filled with smoke. The mistake would be to try to feel that you have to be sorry. No, sorrow is everywhere around you and yet you are free from it.

If we imagine that the air is filled with sorrow, then we can do anything we like in it. We can move, we can speak, we can sit quietly, but we must try to be in harmony with this imaginary atmosphere. This is also very easy. It is only difficult if we try to force ourselves to feel sorrow. This is wrong.

Now try to imagine how you must move in order to be in harmony with this imaginary atmosphere. If you have trained your body by means of other exercises, you will be able to move in harmony with this atmosphere of sorrow. And as soon as you begin to produce these simple movements, there begins to be something inside you like a life, which can be called, "I am sorry." Without any reason. In our art we don't have to have reasons. As soon as we have to have reasons, we can do nothing with them, and then it is not art. The actor must be able to cry without any reason, simply because he is an actor. If he cannot cry immediately, then he must leave the stage. If he has to recall the death of his father, poor old man, etc., etc., then he is not an actor. If I can be angry without any reason, then I am an actor, but if I have to think of Himmler, whom I hate, before I can be angry, then I am not an actor. Everything has to be at my disposal because everything is developed.

As soon as we imagine the atmosphere and imagine it in the air around us, and then move in it in harmony, then our feelings will arise, and we can act with pleasure. The next step will be to radiate back this atmosphere. We have to increase it, because if we get something from a certain inspiration, there is nothing for us to do but to give it back—to mirror it. Atmosphere has the ability to be increased to a very great extent if we are able to send it out.

Here again is a very subtle point. We can egotistically enjoy the atmosphere and keep it for ourselves, but it will immediately die out. Whereas, the more we give it back, the more it will increase. But because all actors in all countries are to a certain extent egotistical, they are afraid of the audience. They depend upon the opinion of the audience, and this egotistical contraction and fear before the audience is so great that we cannot mirror anything and all our efforts are only "pushing," with our words, with our faces, with our clichés, because we are afraid of the audience. Instead of letting the audience collaborate with us and then it will be "our" performance, working together because the atmosphere is there.

The significance of atmosphere in our time is perhaps more important than anything else because I think the theatre is, and will be, one of the most important cultural mediums for present humanity. Because the atmosphere, just as it opens our own hearts if we imagine it around us, it opens the hearts of everyone in the audience. And if we, through our profession, are able to open the hearts of our fellow men we shall create a miracle. Because the thing which we lack so much is feelings in our life, and if we want to serve our present time, it does not mean that we necessarily have to take a modern play, about modern times, just written. We can take a play written hundreds of years ago, if we are able by means of this play to awaken human beings to things which are sitting so deeply inside them—things which we keep so closed and suppressed that we cannot understand the things which are going on around us. We cannot understand the war in Europe, we cannot understand what is coming to us, what is going to happen, what will be the end of Hitler, we cannot understand anything because we do not feel it. But we must understand. When the heart is torn to pieces and is open and the intellect becomes a servant, then we immediately see what Hitler is, what he has already got, what we cannot avoid, what we can avoid—all these social, cultural problems can be solved by the means of our beautiful, mysterious, great profession, the theatre. And the atmosphere is the means by which we can speak to the audience about things without using words to speak to, to listen to.

Many years ago I tried the following *experiment* while acting Hamlet. I tried to act Hamlet each night not as I wanted to, but as the audience wanted me to. It was very interesting because each evening I got different suggestions and questions, as it were, from the audience. If it was an audience from the street, I got one thing. If it was a group of teachers, I got quite another lot of questions, and they had to be answered differently. And so on. So I am absolutely positive that if the atmosphere is there, the audience will tell us so many things and we shall tell them so many things which *they* really need and which *we* really need and our time needs—only by means of atmosphere.

And here again is a very interesting thing. In the present theatre we rely very much on the meaning of the word and we speak from the stage the content, the meaning, the "what," and, therefore, we don't need as if any atmosphere, because we can say the "what" without any atmosphere. But as soon as the atmosphere is there, let us say the atmosphere of love, you will presently forget the meaning and speak something much more. Our language, our words, will become so full of "meaning," which is more than "content." And if we speak these loving words in the atmosphere of hatred, for instance, it is a very interesting combination, a collision of things which makes it interesting. Superhuman, under-human, anything but the bare thing itself.

So the atmosphere is the best director. No director can suggest things which the atmosphere can, and if it is there and the actors are agreed upon certain atmospheres and really create them, you will find that you are acting tonight not just as you acted yesterday—it will be different because the atmosphere is the life and the life is never the same. On the stage we will find such a variety of things inside us if we become inspired by atmospheres we create ourselves.

Now, let me finish my comparison of the performance as an independent being, with the human being. The performance is the idea, the "what," the realm of feelings, the atmosphere, and the will. Everything which we can see on the stage with our eyes, everything that is audible, belongs to the realm of the will of the performance. It moves, it is there, it is a constant process. And if we shall define these three things, we shall find later on the place where and how to apply certain points of the method.

THE OBJECTIVE

Let us take an example from Stanislavsky's Method—the objective. Very often actors try by mistake to apply the objective to the realm of ideas—it cannot be applied there—it has to be applied to the realm of the will, because the objective is that which I am going to *do*, to act, that which I *want*. We need only move inwardly to the objective, and be still outwardly, because inwardly we are always moving. While sitting there, if you realize it, you will find you are moving inwardly. I can move visibly with my hands, my body, my eyes, and I can also move only inwardly, and that is the realm of the objective.

RADIATION

Of course, we can take another point—radiation. Consciously radiate so that you feel that you are giving out everything you can to your audience. Of course, it has to do with the will very much, but you can radiate your feelings. It is the realm of the heart.

If this division of thought, feeling, and will seems to be intellectual and dry, it only seems to be because when you feel that you can really manage these three levels concretely, you can plunge into the realm of ideas, or become absolutely filled with the realm of feelings. You can live in the realm of the heart, as well as in the realm of the will. When you feel it concretely and it is no longer an abstract idea, which it seems to be in our talk today, when it becomes concrete, then you will see that all these things are the means of expression, are tools in our profession, and this temporary anatomizing will lead us later on to such a composition of things in us, such a harmonious composition, that we shall be able to discover in ourselves many things which want to be awakened but we don't allow them, because of the chaos which is going on in our actor's nature while we are preparing the play.

DEVELOPING THE ACTOR'S NATURE

Now, the last thing for today. The way to develop our own nature takes time. We have to use a certain amount of time and effort for training ourselves, but after this period of training which may be a long one, we will find it a real economy of time. Sometimes this period of training is mistaken in our profession for a loss of time, when we have to produce plays in four weeks. We think that if this training takes years there must be something wrong. The wrong is only if we think the period of training is an eternal one. No. It is a long one, but when it is accomplished it is such an economy of time. When you can laugh, cry, sing, be happy at once—when you have trained your imagination so that you can see the whole of *Othello* at once—that is real economy of time.

If we don't have to keep our hands in our pockets for the first two weeks before we overcome our sense of shame, we will realize what our hands and arms can do for us as means of expression. If we are free to move our hands and arms from our center and not from our joints and are free, then we can speak of economy of time. So really it is the greatest economy of time to spend a long period of time in training. When everything is there, after a long period of training, then I will believe that the performance can be done even in two weeks. But not now.

Second Class

Questions and Answers

November 11, 1941

ATMOSPHERE

Does the actor create the atmosphere out of the objects, or is it a separate entity?

The actor must imagine the air filled with the atmosphere which has been decided upon. Therefore, it is the actor's work.

With regard to the atmosphere of the street accident—when the quantitative change takes place, the qualitative one takes place also.

INFLUENCES

On the street it is done unconsciously, but on the stage we must create certain atmospheres consciously, in order that we will get what we want. But I also believe that there is something more to it—*a certain influence* from somewhere else which we do not know about. I believe this. I mean that there are influences around us in the world which cannot be found out by analysis or any psychological means. Certain influences on which we depend more than we think, and the atmosphere is just an instance of these influences being strong enough for us to realize them, without being able to say what it is or where it comes from.

But if we don't understand them, we can't use them.

Of course we can. These "influences" are longing to come to us, and if we call them by means of creating the atmosphere consciously, "they" are here. They are not running away from us—they are coming to us and trying to influence us in all possible ways. But they cannot reconcile themselves with our intellect—that stops them. But if we are open in our hearts and wills, and the intellect is a servant, then they are here to help us.

Can you make it a little clearer, even though we are speaking of intangible things?

Two things always happen in such cases. If you close yourself, the influence of these "beings," let us say, is lessened. Secondly, he who closes himself to the influence of these "beings" excludes himself, so that both parts are suffering somehow. This disharmony affects both parts. This does not mean that if we submit to the atmosphere we have to feel just what the atmosphere dictates. We have to have personal feelings which are different but still the general atmosphere is there. However, if you reject it, it cannot force itself on you.

Let us imagine an atmosphere—created by us as actors—in which we are waiting for somebody to enter the room, somebody who is very unpleasant. The moment we begin to lie, everything disappears. Now imagine we are waiting in a tense, unpleasant atmosphere. If we are true, the atmosphere is there, but the moment we begin to lie and exaggerate, it disappears immediately. So there is one absolute condition—it must be true, otherwise there is no contact between the actors themselves or between this "influence" and the actors.

It seems to me that the atmosphere is a result of something you achieve from something you have done. Through really doing something the atmosphere is achieved. So as an actor what is important to me is that I am really doing.

Yes. Imagining the air filled with atmosphere is also *doing*—the *doing* must absolutely be there. *Doing* is absolutely important on the stage.

You have said that if we allow the dry, cold intellect to creep in, it would kill the performance. When writing the play, the playwright must have an idea—that is the thing which forces him to write. So the actor must understand what he is doing in terms of the content of the play and the part. Also he must be clear intellectually about what he is doing on the stage. But I gather that is not the cold, dry intellect of which you speak.

THE INTELLECT

Of course the actor must know everything he possibly can. But the difference is *how* he knows it. That is the whole difference between the cold intellect and another kind of thinking which does not disturb the actor. The cold intellect is the kind in which we do not see anything but facts. But if our "knowledge" is at the same time an imaginative picture, then everything is all right because all real imagination is filled with emotions and will-impulses, and the intellect is still in the position of a servant who carries a candle, and does nothing but throw light.

Otherwise I feel that although you might react in general to what was going on, it would become vague and diffused.

Emotions without anything to direct them are even more terrible than doing things by means of the cold intellect. The intellect must be turned into a vision.

Is the intellect more like a rationalizing—a very intellectual process which you don't participate in, and which does not flow into the three levels of experience.

Of course. I have meant just what you described.

The actor must not be a critic. If you use the intellect only, you are not creating.

The main disturbing thing in our meaning of "intellect" is that we think of it as analyzing, criticizing, or punishing. It is a negative thing. The Russian word means just "rationalizing." It is much narrower than the intellect.

But I also think if our "knowledge" and understanding of what we are *doing* on the stage is developed—the more we really understand in the good sense so that our imagination is awakened and we see things immediately—then a strange thing happens. The more we know, the more subconscious or super-conscious things are coming upon us, so there is no danger. The subconscious region opens itself.

I think it is important to clarify these terms. I have always felt this, and the other day Stark Young confirmed my belief when he explained to me that we have to go through this stage of confusion until we find out what we actually mean when we speak about "atmosphere," "feelings," "intellect," etc., so it is useful to define the terms we are going to use.

I am not completely sure of what you mean by "will impulses."

THE WILL

Of course I must come back again to the same themes from different points of view. About the will; in our sense it is a very simple thing. It is nothing other than the anticipation of what shall happen, and that is at the same time the objective—not quite as it is described by Stanislavsky who invented it, but with a little nuance which I suggest.

THE OBJECTIVE

I suggest that we do not try to find out the objective as the pure understanding of what we want to do, but to see the result achieved. That is the objective for me and that is the *will* on the stage. If I want to shake hands with someone, for instance, I may say that I want to shake hands with her, but if I don't see myself doing it, then how shall I do it? Then it is the intellect. But if I *see* that I am shaking hands, then I see a picture which leads my will. To anticipate, to foresee, that is the real objective.

When I was a young actor under Stanislavsky, I could not realize this difference for a long time. Then I realized that I must always have a picture before me, and after that, all went well. I would also add to this not to try to find the objective before first acting freely. First act freely, even badly, and then ask yourself, "What have I done?" Then you can correct it, and also with the intellect, etc. This is the way to find the objective.

When starting an objective, if you feel very flat and don't know how to get warm, it helps to take an objective which has some connection with the whole scene.

THE IMAGINATION

It may help very much in your case, but in this case, I would say that you should choose the most simple, the most obvious objective. The easiest way to get the objective, and, at the same time, to become warm is to appeal to our imagination. For instance, let us take Sir Toby entering the cellar in *Twelfth Night*. If I can see him entering the cellar in my imagination then I can find the objective. If I cannot see him, then I am not an actor. When I see him, immediately the objective will come. It can be developed, of course, but it must always be a kind of vision. Nobody else in the world can see my Sir Toby, just as no one can see himself. The imagination is nearer to us, and is what leads us soonest to the stage which we may call "to be warm" or to be ready to act.

I always feel very unhappy when someone says, "But that is not Shakespeare!" How do we know what Shakespeare thought or saw? I have my Shakespeare and you have yours—no one has the right to criticize it.

But does it not seem that we develop certain associations around certain images, for example, a fat Santa Claus? It seems to me that the whole problem of the cultural image is something we are afraid of.

We make one big mistake—we discard one thing or the other, whereas both are true. Santa Claus is there, even if one has a beard a bit shorter and the other a bit longer.

You speak about and demonstrate the ideal actor who can laugh or cry at will. You say it is not necessary for the developed, mature actor to think of his "dying grandfather." It makes sense to me, but I don't know how, although I have understood everything you have said about what we want to achieve—the goal. But perhaps I have to use my "dying grandfather" because that is the only way I can get at the goal I want. My problem is, what should I use in place of my "dying grandfather"?

There are two things with which we can replace the "dying grandfather." First of all, a developed, flexible, emotional life. If it is developed, it includes all the "grandfathers" in existence. We don't need any one particular image. In it are all "Lears," all "fathers," all everything—if the emotional life is developed, it is there forever. That is one thing. There is another way, but it seems to me a little dangerous. If we take the real image of our real grandfather, it becomes too personal in the wrong sense. You will get certain feelings, perhaps strong ones, but they will be of a different kind than we are aiming at in our work—they are not to be shown. They will have a certain personal color which makes us a little smaller and makes the audience suspicious whether consciously or unconsciously, and the actor can become hysterical after a certain period of time if he works in this way, because we do not allow our nature to forget the "grandfather" drama in our life to the extent that our psychological life requires. We always take him out of his grave and cannot forget him, which makes us psychologically ill after a time, because we force our nature.

If an actor has a very strong imagination, that imagination is all inclusive. One does not have to depend on a specific incident, but one can gather that feeling from many incidents. Our problem in creating feelings lies in the inability to really concentrate to the point where the imagination is strong, without being disturbed. If our concentration is so strong that we can actually and truly imagine, our responses would be stronger.

From my point of view this is absolutely right.

What I am driving at is this. You, for example, are a mature actor, but that is not true of me. Some things I can do, others not. What I am trying to find out is how to deepen this experience and manage that place where I am not so strong. One way may be through the experience of my "dying grandfather." What I am looking for is a concrete way to overcome these weak spots in me. You may say concentrate more, but that is not right for me. When it does not happen for me, what do I do then?

The imagination of an actor is not that of an ordinary person. I want to know how to do things which I am not able to do.

What I understand is this. We have all relied on our "grandfathers" and our personal lives in relation to a part, instead of fully exploring the play itself. Instead of doing that, we have relied on our personal feelings. If we concentrated and worked upon the imaginative possibilities of the characters in the play, it would come.

We are all here because we want you to show us a way by which we can go away from you better actors.

Is it true that you mean that there is a technical equipment which makes it possible for me to use all the "grandfathers"?

I understand what you mean but I cannot do it. Perhaps I was not born an emotionally developed person. I have tried to find my way to it and the first step is to turn to the things I know best—or whatever image moves me.

You use the phrase "a flexible emotional life." I have tried to remember something which made me laugh or cry, and I have not been successful. Later on I was able to do it. If I trace it, I find that in life I have been differently moved in different experiences, and this has worked into my technique as an actor.

CONCENTRATION

The moment I begin to concentrate on the object I begin to use my imagination, and it becomes something else.

That is the thing we are aiming at. If by concentrating our imagination is arous- ed, then we have achieved our purpose.

I don't think that is true.

The purpose of concentration seems to be going out of oneself, but actually it is going into oneself so deeply that you will find all your abilities trembling and willing to obey. Concentration alone is opening the door of your own creative ability. You can direct this the way you want, but it may happen that it will be the way to your own creative individuality. Nobody knows what it is but you yourself.

This may cover all your questions. First of all, it seems to me that there is no contradiction in our understanding of the theatre. The whole difference is that you say that when you think of your "dying grandfather," he leads you to big- ger things. This is just the opposite to what I have just said, which is that it makes you smaller. If we accumulate enough experiences from our "grand- fathers" and then forget them, we will not need to remember our "grand- fathers." You need only to remember the atmosphere, to have a spark of an- ticipation of what it should be, laughter, sorrow, and so on. The same "grand- father," if he has been forgotten and gone his way, will return as an artistic emotion. I am speaking against remembering things which are still *too personal.*

The whole question is, can we develop in ourselves the power of imagination and concentration. I am sure we can. Therefore, the whole question is, are we going to develop them? If we do, it means that we move towards the aim which is actually the same one. But the question is, can we take one step nearer to the ability not to remember our "grandfather" or do we still have to remember him? If we can only remember him and nothing else, then we are not artists. But we assume that we are artists, and the question only remains whether we want to develop certain abilities or not.

Here I think that the ability to concentrate is a very important point. Unless we develop this special ability we cannot accumulate many things, and we don't see many things because the life does not enrich us to the extent that we need. Without this golden key we cannot do very much. Nothing can be done without this special kind of concentration.

If, for instance, we imagine King Lear, we can imagine him only because we are already rich enough inside ourselves with all the "grandfathers" which we have forgotten. But we cannot imagine King Lear if we have concrete grand- father who is still tearing our physical nerves and heart to pieces. Concentra- tion makes us accumulate more "grandfathers," and digest them more quickly.

When my own father was dying I concentrated my attention on him to such an extent that, although it was very tragic and painful to me, I digested the whole event to such an extent that I could use it in *King Lear*—in fact, I had to use it. If I had not completely concentrated at the moment of my father's death,

I might have dragged it with me for many years, and been unable to use it sub-consciously. When I cry, I am, of course, crying for my father, my mother, my dog, and all those things and people whom I have actually forgotten, but they are crying through me.

So it is just a question of concentration. If we are able to concentrate to such an extent, and by the means which we will work upon, then the ability to laugh, to cry, to be influenced by one's own imagination will come more quick-ly, and more easily. It is only a question of developing and training.

I believe that we are all more talented than we seem to be. Actually I believe that we are all geniuses, but we don't know it, and we are afraid of it and believe that we cannot do this or that, because of inhibitions, under-developed imaginations, etc., therefore, we have to use clichés. If one thinks back over one's own life, one will find moments when there are signs of genius. For the ex-perienced actor it is only a question of cleaning one's own inner life by the right means, with patience and great effort, then we will discover many things which we cannot even believe are there.

How can we, for instance, dream such strange things—such strange interplay of characters, atmospheres and emotions—we cannot do it if we think we can only do this and no more. We must say to ourselves that we can do much more, if we only discard certain things and develop others. Of course, it takes time, which is unpleasant, but we have to pay for the result.

I think we all desire to hear from you a simple system of technique for doing certain things. You have said something which I feel is an answer to this question of technique, and I would like to explore it further. That is the idea of conceiving the finished picture before it is finished. I was warned against this in the previous work I have done, but it attracts me and I like it. It seems to tie up with your other conception of the will im-pulses, which I think is a much larger development of the idea of the objective. I would like to have that developed further, because for me that is the "how."

As long as we have to *speak* about this method, it will seem a little difficult, because we have to *do* it in order to understand. But when you come to do it, you will find that it is very simple. All the points I have mentioned one by one are really brothers and sisters and are actually one thing. There is really only one button you have to press inside, and all these brothers and sisters will become alive, but to become acquainted with them you must speak with each one individually. Actually, it is a very simple method. We will come to the point where we have spoken about so many things—concentration, imagina-tion, radiation, atmosphere, and so on. Just the same is true of atmosphere; when you want atmosphere and really create it, then everything else is there. It is one thing. So a great mathematician may arrive at a certian mathematical formula, after many years of writing many formulas which he could not bring together. Suddenly it comes, and this pleasant moment is inevitable.

EXERCISES IN CONCENTRATION

Very often in theatre schools, we start by using two main organs—the eyes and ears. For a certain stage in our work that is all right but we must go further. Let us say we want to concentrate on some object. We have to see it, and that is the first stage. We can even describe it in details to support what we see with our eyes. Then we must do the following things: without moving physically, we must move our whole being towards the object. For instance, when we love, we concentrate on the person to such an extent that we are continuously moving towards that person. So by our will we must move inwardly towards the object of our concentration. The physical body remains quiet but something moves towards this object. When you are *with* the object, the physical body must remain free and relaxed. Then you will feel that your looking and seeing is of secondary importance.

Now you have the object not with your eyes only, but with something else which is much more important, much more "taking" the thing, than with your eyes. The last step is to "take" the object and keep it—to such an extent that you will not know whether the object has you, or you have the object—you become one with it. And when you become one, a miracle happens—you know exactly how heavy it is, what shape it is, what noise it makes, what shape it is from all sides at the same time. With our eyes we see the surface. When we approach the object with our physical body we know it somehow vaguely, when we "take" it, we know it better, and when we are "taken" by it, all the qualities of the thing we know and experience. Take two objects—the more we do this process of merging together with these things, the more different they become until they are incomparable, and they can show us so much that we may even become frightened, but it is the only real way to *know* things. This process of concentration, of "merging" together, is the only way to really *know* things. Whether it is a box of matches or a human being, the process of concentration, of merging together without the physical body is the same. Whether it is the Moses" of Michaelangelo, a real person, a sound in the street, etc., the power f concentration has to be just the same in all cases.

If we are able to get so many interesting things from simple objects, how much more enriching and interesting will be the work on the part we are going to play. We can concentrate on our part if we are able to concentrate to the point where we no longer need to look at the object. Then it makes no difference whether it is an imaginary character—Sir Andrew Aguecheek, or the actor whom I see on the stage with body and costume. The imagination becomes so concrete and through the power of concentration makes immediately the world of imagination so real and concrete that there is no need to remember the real "grandfather," because the imaginary "grandfather," which is shown the actor as King Lear, Claudius, etc., etc., is just as concrete. More than that it is so free from the actor's nerves and physical pain, which is not so if I think of my not-forgotten father or mother or grandfather.

THE IMAGE

This begins to show us how much it is all one thing—concentration makes imagination concrete, and imagination, if it is concrete, cannot be produced without concentration of this kind. Another and last result of this exercise will be that the images which we are going to act by such kind of concentration and highly developed imagination, will appear before us while we are working on the part. They will appear before us absolutely concretely, so that although we cannot see them with our physical eyes, we can describe the spot on which Hamlet stands, the wrinkles in his face, etc., etc. These will come of themselves. I know of one case when an actor was reading a book which had nothing to do with the part he was working on. Suddenly he felt "he is here," but the book interested him, and he did not want to look at the image. There was a real fight between them, but the image was so strong that the actor stopped reading and gave in to the image. The power of such imagination is incredible. It is stronger than a real person, because the means by which this image insists on merging with the actor is of such a nature that he cannot say "no" to it.

But the means to this imagination is to develop this kind of concentration which is by going out of one's physical body as it were, and "taking" the image, the thing, or the sound, and merging with it. While exercising, it is important not to allow oneself to break the concentration—of course, it will happen but then one gets to the point where one can grasp the image and keep it without breaking the connection. Let us do it by concentrating on the object and being *with* it. Then we can go on smoking and talking, and still we will have an unbroken connection with the thing.

CONCENTRATION

I can force myself to concentrate on the simple qualities of the matchbox, but actually I only find it intersting if it is related to something else which arouses my interest and excitement. I cannot get excited about it unless it is more than just the simple object.

If it, the object, remains only the object, then this is not experiencing a developed concentration. This becomes an intellectual thing of observing and watching.

These are only two variations of what happens when you are really concentrated. But there are many more. In the process of real concentration, you experience many things before you are able to pursue your aim. You will meet so many things that it will seem that each one is different, but there are so many rooms to be gone through before you get a real grasp on concentration. One day you can go one way, and the next day another, and each time you will find different ways—all are true. For instance, you may start with a simple object some time, and suddenly you will see your own immediate future, and you will think you are crazy, but because you are going so deeply into yourself you see yourself in the future, in the past, etc. On the other hand, you can really remain with the image, and can do so well that you are almost "taking" it. From the beginning, it may seem different, but it is always the same.

I think concentration means something else. I feel that my concentration would be dissolved if I allowed myself to go further than that.

If you have the *power* of concentration—which is not the object at all—it is what comes to you *through* the power of concentration that we are aiming at. You must distinguish inwardly whether you are floundering, or whether your concentration on a certain object has led you somewhere where you want to go. It depends on you. From your experience you will know whether you are floundering.

What is the proof of concentration, when you have such a varied collection of experiences? How do you know if we are concentrating?

I cannot know whether you are concentrating, but there are certain symptoms which show it.

And whatever happens as a result will tell you?

Yes. As a practical suggestion, I would say let *everything* happen. Let it be right or wrong, and don't worry about it. Have only one aim—to go out, to grasp, to merge and to hold. After a few days it will become obvious, but the only aim is to concentrate in the way I have suggested. All the symptoms are there because of the attempt to concentrate the attention, as we mean it. All these questions will disappear in time.

This may have something to do with day-dreaming. I have been told that this is wrong, but you say that it is right. If you concentrate to the point where the situation becomes so concrete that you actually feel it and respond to it, then is your concentration right?

Not quite. It is the ability to flounder, but not yet the ability to concentrate. The ability of concentration is the ability to exercise your will. You will not confuse it with day-dreaming, because if you are only drawn into imaginary things, you are the victim, and not the hero. Is it your own will to concentrate and then to follow the thread, or are you led weakly by accidental imagination?

Day-dreaming is not concentration as we mean it. When I told you that the part can appear before you even against your will, it is not day-dreaming, but it is because of a strongly developed imagination and concentration. The image comes filled with your own will, therefore you cannot fight it. If you will do the exercises you will see how many things will become quite clear, because of the effort to concentrate alone. Very soon you will be able to distinguish between right and wrong.

I am not clear on the purpose of concentration. It seems to me that when I try to concentrate, the purpose is to release whatever can happen. Probably nothing much hap-

pens as a result of this communion, but it shows that one is waking up inside.

It is true, but there is a danger. Let us imagine, for instance, that someone is going to hypnotize another person. For this, one needs a very strong concentration, and you can't do it if you are not able to *see* the person *doing* the thing. If you are doing this thing by means of the person, then he immediately gets up and does it. But in the middle you may think about his sister, and while you are still in the process of concentration, the purpose is lost. It is a question of your own inner household—what you are aiming at. You may want to flounder a little—then flounder. You may order yourself to remain with the object—then you can remain.

It is your business how you use this power of concentration. You may want to have a very strong imagination about something. You concentrate on the image and follow it. Another time you concentrate for quite another aim—you radiate your feelings from the stage. You can use it for establishing contact with your partners, and you can use it when you first enter the stage for hinting to your audience what will happen to the hero at the end of the play. By means of strong concentration you can tell them what will happen at the end. For instance, if I am playing King Lear—I am earthy and unbridled at the beginning, but I can send one spark to the audience, and they will anticipate the moment of "Howl, howl, howl!"

For all these "tricks" you *must* use concentration. Nothing can be done without it, but, of course, dangers are there too. Instead of following one line you may begin to flounder. All these dangers will become very obvious, if you have the patience to go on in spite of the seeming difficulties.

I feel there is a great difference among the people in this room as to levels of concentration, but we have no basis for knowing how good our concentration is. There should be something more to it, it seems to me. You should be able to get from us, by analysis of some kind, just how good our concentration is.

This is a case in which my help is less and less needed, because the effort to concentrate will itself teach you much more than I can tell you. Of course, I can give you a series of different exercises, but to experience them is something else. For instance, take an imaginary chair and then try to transform the chair—without breaking your attention—into a cow. Very difficult! Terribly difficult! Or imagine that you are pouring tea into a cup, and then try to imagine it reversed. Try to imagine yourself walking backwards. In reality, it is not difficult to do, but in the imagination you need a terrific power of concentration to be able to do it.

If your head gets tired when you are doing these exercises, then it is wrong. Real concentration does not occupy the brain at all, so when the head gets tired don't go further. The more we attempt to go out to the object, the more we will get the feeling that the head has nothing to do with it. Real mathematicians are calculating without using their brains. They are working with different parts of their beings, with different qualities. Only when one is learning arithmetic is one tired. They play chess with their hands and feet, and inaudible voices, etc. So only the first stage of the exercises occupies the physical brain, and it must not become over-tired. Again, let us take the example of love. You cannot be tired of love, if it is a happy one. You will be more and more inspired by it. Just so with concentration. When it is right, you will become more young and strong.

I have in mind a sketch. Let us try to do it with a general atmosphere to begin with, and then we will divide it more and more, and then certain simple situations will develop and this sketch will grow of itself, and will become a play. We will start to create really from nothing, and we will start with it next time. Then I will tell you why we take the opposite way, starting from nothing, so that it will be our own creation.

Third Class

How Shall We Develop Our Emotions and Our Bodies

November 14, 1941

THE CREATIVE INDIVIDUALITY
AND THE "LAYMAN BEING"

How shall we develop our emotions and our bodies? At the moment when we believe that there is a creative individuality, and another whom we call the "layman being," we are already taking part in this fight to accept the creative individuality, and try with it to defeat the "layman" who uses and abuses our voice, body and emotions. This is the moment when you must decide whether you want to go on that way or go on by developing yourself in the school, and in our discussions.

When we realize that there are two individualities—one against the creative process and another for it—then that knowledge alone is already of very great importance. When we know that there are two, and we know which we accept and which we deny, that is already great strength which we can give to the creative individuality, and can weaken the "layman" in us. As soon as we begin to develop our bodies, voices, and emotions, we begin to get our professional actor's technique, and as soon as we have our technique, we can start the creative process—and what will it be?

ATMOSPHERE

When the creative individuality begins to create, begins to be active, what happens first of all? First of all, the creative individuality feels itself as if surrounded by the atmosphere of future work—we may not yet know what it will be—but we know that our creative individuality is surrounded by a certain definite atmosphere which is pleasantly worrying us. When we have got a certain part and we say we don't like it—why? It is because the atmosphere is of a different kind, and it cannot accept this part. Whether we are conscious of this general atmosphere or not does not mean anything, but we know the result when the atmosphere says, "No, it is not what I want." Or we can say, for instance, that we want to act more tragic parts, more melodramatic parts, etc. What does it mean? It is a general atmosphere which one carries with one for one's whole life as a creative individuality. So there is a general atmosphere which dictates to us, as actors, what we have to act.

Of course, there are individuals who have many atmospheres which change with the years, with the times, the day, etc., but still there is one individual atmosphere always present. For instance, one wants to be a clown but has never had this opportunity, and this atmosphere of clown remains unsatisfied. This was my case. I never had the opportunity to show all those clown tricks. I wanted to be a clown, but I was acting Hamlet and other parts like that, and there was no place for clowning. Later on I noticed that I was clowning in a modified way![1]

We have to satisfy these atmospheres and we cannot avoid it. To kill an atmosphere which surrounds an individual is impossible. We have to feel it and when we know that there are atmospheres always in us, surrounding us, then again the knowledge of it makes a great difference in our own lives. If I know I am a clown, it makes life easier for me.

TECHNIQUE OF READING THE TEXT

Each *creation* starts with *atmosphere*, however hidden and obscure it may be, it always starts with the atmosphere. Therefore, if we receive a part, and start with the text and begin to study the part with the ideas and thoughts and events and logical succession of facts, which are given in the play, we do, to my mind, the greatest mistake because we start from the point which is not logically right for a creative process. We start with the very thing with which we have to finish. We have to *finish* with the written play—that will be the result when we are so far advanced in our part. We shall be able to read it and understand what is behind it, and must not start with the superficial understanding of who is speaking to whom, what about, and what shall happen. This approach makes us somehow dry, dull, and professional in the wrong way, and kills the atmosphere not only of this special play, but our own atmospheres, whatever they are, are somehow offended.

If we start with the reading of the text, I feel I understand the play, but I lose myself. The more I read the play, the text, the more I *understand* it, the more I lose the interest for acting, and I begin to think of the production, what costumes I shall wear, how much I will get, and how I will get rid of the rehearsals as soon as possible. Not because we are not artists, but because we start with the wrong thing which offends the most profound thing—our individuality, surrounded by atmospheres.

What should we actually do? We should start with reading the play, but overlooking the thoughts, the logic of everything and to, first of all, throw away everything I have known about the play. Before we start to work on *Romeo and Juliet*, we have to throw away everything we have known about it, and start anew by starting to enjoy the atmospheres. Read it again and again, scene after scene. As soon as you can satisfy your hunger for the atmosphere of the play, every kind of reading is right and even no reading is right.

THE CREATIVE INDIVIDUALITY—THE ARTIST

I have prepared a little chart:

1. The creative individuality is high above everything, and our undeveloped part is down here.
2. Then comes the creative individuality surrounded by the atmospheres.
3. Then our technique comes when we try to satisfy our necessity for atmosphere.

IMAGINING THE PLAY

When, for instance, we are going to produce *Romeo and Juliet*, we, first of all, read the play several times and create in our minds and souls the atmosphere. Then the next step will be given—while reading the play—which is to see, to imagine—not to understand—but to *imagine* the text. This is much more pleasant than to read and memorize the lines. To imagine all the events, characters, etc., whether they are very fine, or whether they are primitive at the very beginning, it does not matter, the only important thing is that we avoid the mistake of never imagining the play.

When you imagine the balcony scene, for instance, you will imagine all the pictures you have seen. You will be disturbed by the many pictures, but you will eventually get rid of them.

The third stage is to imagine the whole play—one sentence, one word, details, etc. This kind of imagination will be prompted entirely by the atmosphere. All the images which will come, whether primitive or complicated, will be in full harmony with the atmosphere of *Romeo and Juliet*, which we will have discovered or created while reading the play.

Now the process of atmosphere. It must go on simultaneously with our everyday rehearsals. We have to adjust ourselves to it. By imagining *Romeo and Juliet*, and especially your own part in it, you have to try to develop in more and more detail everything you are going to perform. The more details the better. That means that you have to *act* in your imagination, your own part, and also act other parts as much as you need in order to clarify your own part, your own character, etc.

THE ACTOR AS DIRECTOR

Every actor must be a director, at least inwardly. The psychology of the director must be known to each actor. That means that the actor who gets a part must be able to see everything around this part. He must be able to see the whole performance, or at least to anticipate how he would produce the play. The Broadway producer will produce a play his own way, quite differently from us, but it is a harmless contradiction.

The important thing is that we have an eye which sees more than just our own part. While imagining *Romeo and Juliet* and your own part, you have to more or less imagine the whole performance around you. It will become necessary, because the atmosphere of *Romeo and Juliet* will not allow you to confine yourself only to your own character. It has to be done in order to satisfy the atmosphere which becomes more and more creative and demanding. To satisfy such an atmosphere, one has to imagine everything.

THE CREATIVE INDIVIDUALITY

That is what happens schematically. First, the creative individuality surrounded by the atmosphere, and then into the atmosphere you put more and more images and details. The first thing was our undeveloped emotions and body. Then when we begin to develop the general technique, something rises up as if to meet the imaginative performance. When the imagination is being developed more and more in details, you will need not only a good general technique, but a special technique for a special part. The technique for Don Quixote is different than that for Faust, the technique for King Lear is different than the technique for Cordelia. This is the most pleasant thing for our creative individuality—which is the artist in us.

This special technique needs to be found each time we prepare a part. For instance, we must find out how King Lear walks, because no one in the world walks like him. How Ophelia walks is again the thing which must be found by the actor. This special technique, this special body for King Lear, this special voice.

THE ACTOR'S VOICE

The greatest mistake we make is that we always use our own voices for every part. Lack of imagination, lack of interest for the character, lack of time, perhaps, but it gives one of the poorest impressions of our present theatre. We speak "in general" and so much in the one tone that we have lost the feeling for the voice—only thoughts, business, ideas. We don't hear our own voices speaking, or our fellow-man speaking. We don't really *hear* much either—we understand much but we don't hear. But if one's voice changes suddenly, we realize that it is not the usual voice. On the stage it is actually our duty to produce a new voice for each part. When we act Cordelia and Ophelia and Maria with our own voice, it is wrong theatrically.

From the artistic point of view, if we will listen to the character speaking, we will discover that we cannot hear this voice—how she acts and how she speaks is in great disharmony—someone else speaks from behind her. One actor speaks wrongly, another moves wrongly, and another forces his emotions wrongly. But by imagining in detail and by hearing the voice of Juliet in our imagination, we will get the desire to imitate this fine voice which we hear in our imagination. Then we have to appeal to our own voice to see whether we can produce it, and that is the question of technique.

Then we meet this necessity to have a special technique, a special voice, special body and special composition of emotions. Now the individual becomes more active. The atmosphere surrounds all the images, the images are born, and the general technique becomes a special one.

INSPIRATION

When it happnes that we have elaborated our special technique for this particular part, and when we have by certain means incorporated all our images—by using our special techniques for this character—then we have to wait for the last stage which comes of itself. And this stage is what we call *inspiration..*

Inspiration comes when everything is forgotten—the method, the technique, the part, the author, the audience, everything. Then a miracle happens. It happens that the play, the part, begins to exist independently of ourselves. Everyone knows this pleasant state, which cannot be mistaken by anyone. It is a moment of such greatness and strength that it cannot be mistaken for anything else.

INSPIRED ACTING

It is the moment of inspiration when the character, being prompted by the right atmosphere, being prepared by careful imagining, being friends with the creative individuality is not there and we here. No—the individuality is here and there and everything is one harmonious, well-integrated psychological and physical whole. It is the event for which we have come onto the stage. We have chosen our profession because our artistic individuality has anticipated this inspiration. That is the beginning of our career, the dream of our profession, and it must be the end of our profession. In between is work, technique, effort, and then comes this harmonious whole.

IMPROVISATION

Now I hope you will accept my suggestion that we shall start our sketch as if logically—first the atmosphere, then elaboration and technique, and then comes the moment of inspiration. Therefore, we shall start our sketch with atmosphere. I will give you a certain material for imagining, and we shall study what should be *the logic of a creative process.*

I have in mind a theme which I want to bring to the point of performance. At the moment, I am the only one who knows what it is, but we will gradually come to the performance.

ATMOSPHERES FOR THE SKETCH

The first atmosphere will be the following one: Early morning—very early—before dawn, in a tavern which is very dirty, very low. All the people are very drunk—they have been drinking the whole night. Everyone is tired and exhausted—prostitutes and sailors. Everything that could happen has happened. They are exhausted, unbridled, weak, over-tired—it is like a nightmare. Somewhere there are attempts to sing the songs which have been sung during the night—disharmony everywhere. Satiety. Drinking goes on very lazily—some exclamations, some attempts to sing, nothing reasonable, tired, stuffy. This is the atmosphere.

Try to imagine it around us—don't try to *feel* anything. We will feel as soon as the atmosphere is there. When you imagine the atmosphere around you, allow yourself to be open to it. Don't force yourself to be open—just open yourself to this heavy atmosphere. Now try to move a little in harmony with this atmosphere. In making these small movements, try to avoid analyzing what these movements mean. Without any special aim except to move harmoniously with the atmosphere. Don't allow your intellect to hold you at this moment.

Now, while producing these movements, simply speak the word, "Well," which it must also be in the atmosphere. Then get up, as if to go home, and fall down again. In harmony with the atmosphere. Then someone starts to sing vaguely, others try to join, then drop it. Each sailor and prostitute will choose a partner, and will sit together—they have been together so much physically that they cannot be separated. He: "How long have you been here?" She: "For eight years." Both are absolutely indifferent. Now drop the atmosphere.

Now take the moment when the greatest activity is present—singing, drinking, and kissing each other. This time the atmosphere is that of the same tavern—the same smelly, dirty, low standard of morality. It is night, and all the devils are here. Unbridled atmosphere—very active. It is full of a certain hot love—sly love—no hatred. One sailor, the captain, is in the room with a girl. He tells the sailors that they must be at the boat at six o'clock. They attempt to capture some semblance of *discipline*.

There are two atmospheres for this sketch, which you can exercise at home. Imagine the air around you filled with the atmosphere. Try to move and speak in it—first in one and then in the other.

FEELING OF EASE

There are four qualities which each artist must have developed in himself so strongly that they are always there. Whatever the part, whatever the moments in the part, these four qualities are symptoms of one who is a creative artist. We call it *feeling of ease* because it is a very strongly expressed feeling of lightness and ease.

That means that whatever we are going to experience on the stage—even if it is terribly heavy and uneasy—the impression that it is terribly heavy must be given, but *how* it is produced must be artistically light and easy always. Then it will be really something which we may enjoy, and we will understand much more what is behind the acting which is permeated with this feeling of ease. If, for instance, we show a very heavy thing with a feeling of ease, being light and easy in our muscles and our psychology, it will be pleasant for the audience, but if we are really doing it heavily and tensely—using everything opposite to the feeling of ease—it will give the impression of heaviness, but it will be an unpleasant sensation for the audience. Such efforts make the audience and the actors really ill—if two men are fighting in earnest on the stage, it is impossible to look at, but if they fight having this ability of ease, they will give the impression of a fight, but it will be a work of art.

Let us take the example of Michaelangelo's "Moses." There you will see how heavy is each fold of the cheek, and the nose, and the hair, and the clothes—and at the same time how light. Look at it from this point of view—the most heavy things are expressed with the magic feeling of ease.

Another example: when laborers are at work, they must get this feeling of ease when using their heavy tools. If they did not get this feeling of ease and rhythm, they could not do their work. Nature itself forces them to get immediately this feeling of ease. So this first quality will be useful for all of us. It makes the actor twice as happy on the stage, and the audience three times as happy when watching him. There is no philosophy about it, it is simply a feeling of ease. One is light when in a good mood, and heavy when in a bad mood.

EXERCISE

Try to recall the feeling of your body without weight. Just lift your arm and experience the desire to become easier and lighter. This simple exercise can lead to great results. If we are able to move with a feeling of ease, we are changing our psychology. Many experiences will come as a result of knocking at this door of the feeling of ease. Try to lose the weight of your body.

There is always a certain slight preparation before the movement. Now to this add a certain rhythm which is there by nature. Feel your arms as wings. Now do it twice as quickly, and twice as quickly again. Then do it only in your imagination. When we have no arms and hands at all, when we become accustomed to using our invisible hands and arms, then we will see that we have only to "take" our visible hand with our invisible hands, and it will lose its weight entirely. The *invisible thing* is the *artistic one*. That is feeling of ease.

Now say the word, "Well," with this feeling of ease. That is what carries our speech and makes it much more audible.

Fourth Class

Theory and Practice

November 17, 1941

THEORY AND PRACTICE

Perhaps you will be so kind as to regard all my abstract theoretical talks as things which, if they are really digested, are absolutely practical. If we take them as theory only then, of course, they will be of no use for our professional Broadway work. But if we take them and digest them as suggestions which can permeate everything we are going to do on the stage, then you will be convinced that it is so. Everything depends on how we use these seemingly theoretical things. There are things which are more practical than others. For instance, atmosphere. This can be used by every actor on the stage. Then you will realize that I do not give you anything which is purely theoretical.

EXPRESSIVE OR INEXPRESSIVE ACTING

I will also give you certain means which can apply everywhere—almost like "tricks"—which will make your acting more expressive. My students in our school must not hear about them yet, although actually this is not a "trick," but among us it may become like a "trick" if you will apply it. We know that atmosphere can be applied on the stage, that feeling of ease can and must be applied, and that they will make the acting more expressive. Now I will give you one more thing which will make everything on the stage much more expressive.

Acting becomes less expressive if we forget or neglect one very simple fact which is that the human being—and the actor's being is the increased, enlarged human being—has a certain ability; when doing or speaking something we can stop our speech or action or even our emotions quite abruptly, in order to get as quickly as possible to the next word or business. This abrupt killing or cutting of the word or emotion or action is the thing which makes the human being crippled, but it makes the actor being twice as crippled. The most inexpressive performances are those in which the actors are cutting their words, their emotions, their actions, their business sooner than they should. This little fact makes the acting either expressive or inexpressive. We will try some examples and exercises and you will see what I mean.

Now say the word, "Yes," so that after you have pronounced it something will go on after the word—as if you were making a gesture with your arm and hand. Say the word, "Yes," and then follow with your arm and hand. Then say, "No," with a gesture which follows it. Sustain it. Now just turn your head, as if you have been called.

SUSTAINING

Take another example. Get up from your chair, and continue getting up even after you are already up. This *sustaining* is something which the actor's nature requires. It can become a long and sustained pause. There cannot be a pause on the stage without this sustaining. To be able to hold the pause one has to develop this ability to go on without actually going on. Now say the word, "What," and go on into a long, sustained pause. Try to find enough confidence in yourself so that you can go on sustaining the pause for a long time. You will see how pleasant it is—the "dish" is good, but the "gravy" is the pleasure. This sustaining is the "gravy." Now get up and say the word, "What," and sustain it. It cannot expire because we are actors. The person who is not an actor will not understand what we are talking about, but our actor's nature is longing for this. If we do just the opposite and stop too soon we will be filled with emptiness and shame.

If we develop this ability to go on with what we want, and as long as we want, then we will discover one of the "tricks" I mentioned. Now do it again but this time make it as short as possible, but there must be the idea of sustaining in it. Try to find the difference between cutting the thing abruptly, or having at least one spark of the sustaining. When it involves a long period of sustaining, it is quite clear, but we must have the courage to sustain just for an instant, then the "gravy" is there. This concerns everything we do on the stage, words, emotions, movements, listening, speaking, everything on the stage can be done in this way, and actually should not be done differently. All other dry means are inartistic.

There are moments on the stage when we have to drop our words abruptly, but even then we have to perform as if we have stopped our words abruptly but still there is a little "tail" left for ourselves and the audience. Try saying, "Why are you doing that?" First do it fully and completely and sustain it. Then say, "Why are you. . . ?" and stop as if something had happened—drop the words for the audience but not for yourself. Imagine if I really abruptly drop the words, then I have the impression that nothing is left in the space which I have left. Or I have the illusion that another "I" still lingers and even follows me. That is just what is needed. As actors, we are doing this thing on the stage all the time, and I am only trying to make you aware of the fact. Because I have told you from the beginning that everything is there in our actor's nature, and I have only to point it out for you.

PREPARATION OR ANTICIPATION

The process of sustaining is something which follows our action, speech, etc., but there is another process of sustaining which precedes it, and is just as important. Before I ask, "What," I must already start. Before I speak I must start inwardly—not at once, abruptly and dryly. This we can also do with the gesture. Every little word, or sound, or long speech and business is thus framed by something which is purely an artistic thing which is the air that gives life to everything we do on the stage. Without this preceding and following air or space all things are dry and dead. Let us repeat the exercise with "What." To make it still clearer, precede with the right hand and follow with the left. Now do the same with the exercise of getting up—first the inner gesture of preparation, then get up, then follow with sustaining.

THE PAUSE

The pause on the stage—in the sense that there are no words—may be one which follows a certain action. The pause cannot exist as pause—it is always the result of what has just happened, or it is the preparation for a coming event. Then it is a pause full of theatrical sense. For this we see the pause on the stage falling into several parts. It must be for the continuation of something, or for the preparation of something, and the most beautiful pauses are those which are the continuation of something, and then the turning point of preparation for something new, and a new action. Of course, there are pauses which are only a continuation, and then the pause expires and the action takes place.

EXERCISE

First say, "No," out of which the pause starts as a continuation of the "No," then when I tell you the turning point, prepare it and prepare the word, "Yes," which will be the result of the second part of the pause. Now repeat the exercise: Preparation for "No," sustain, turn the pause, prepare for "Yes," speak and sustain.

If we are filled with certain "tricks," the audience will follow us absolutely without question.

IMPROVISATION

Let us work on the sketch—the scene in the tavern—the series of atmospheres. Like a lot of ants, the people in the tavern are drinking, speaking, moving in the general atmosphere of chaos. 1) Senseless activity—chaos. 2) The atmosphere becomes organized and everyone sings, and all are absorbed in the one song—harmony—excitement, activity, desire to love, etc. 3) The moment when the captain gives the *order*—a short moment of disorganized live, certain *unpleasant* shock. 4) *Intimate life*—intimate talk—secrets—muted—tired and exhausted. This dying out life gives diminuendo—*romantic*. 5) *Scandal—quarrel—fight* between sailor and lover. This breaks up the action between the girl and the sailor—attention—*impending disaster*—long pause. 6) Out of the pause will come *compassion*, which is expressed in the form of *mockery* and teasing the sailor who is crazy and depressed—like an animal who is pursued. This atmosphere is the warmest and most friendly one, but the expression is wrong. For the sailor it is one blow after another, and he does not know how to take it. *Friendly.*

When we start with the right atmosphere and follow it, then lose the atmosphere and follow our acting, having forgotten the atmosphere, it may lead us to the wrong kind of expressiveness. It would be very good if, each time you decide to take the atmosphere, to remind yourself to make sure whether or not the atmosphere is around you. If you will do this and recall the idea of the atmosphere, it will keep you in the right line in your work, whether on Broadway or here in our studio.

FEELING OF EASE

Another thing we have spoken about is the feeling of ease. Now let us repeat some of the exercises. Lift up your arms so that you get the illusion that they are losing their weight. Now kneel. Now add to this the words, "I am getting down," so that the words will be permeated with the feeling of ease. Increase the volume of your voice, but avoid shouting. The feeling of ease will allow you to speak loudly, but it will never be shouting. Shouting on the stage occurs only if you are without the preparation or anticipation, and the sustaining. It will be much more effective if it is produced with the preparation and sustaining, and with the feeling of ease. If you will exercise this, you will see how pleasant it is to speak loudly without shouting.

Now take an oath and produce it with increased volume but without shouting. Now, moving forward, whisper the oath. Then retreat backwards, saying the oath in a whisper. Now vary it by making a very long preparation, then a very short whisper, and sustain. Now a very, very long preparation, a very short oath, and a long sustaining.

Fifth Class

Exercise:
Repetition is the Growing Power

November 21, 1941

It may happen that some of you will wish to make practical use of what we have been talking about, but this is impossible without exercising. Therefore, for those who want to exercise, I will give a suggestion about how to exercise, and what actually the idea of exercise is.

EXERCISE BY REPETITION

We know that rhythm substitutes for power, and that repetition is actually the *growing power*, and herein lies the key to exercise. So to exercise means to do the same thing again and again, and to know that we are doing the same thing again and again is very important, because the psychology of one who exercises is quite different from that of one who exercises without knowing that repetition is actually the growing power.

Therefore, it is so important to start exercising as if anew. That is the secret. Not to have the psychology that I am doing something which becomes somehow stale and dull for me. No. Each time we do the simple lifting and lowering of the arm, do it with a fresh approach and a desire to do it again and again, as if for the first time. This economizes the time and energy very much, because if I think I have done it, and then do it again without any special interest, it is a loss of time and energy. Sometimes we forget this while doing the exercises.

EXERCISE AS ART

Another point, and this is even more important, we must try to get the habit of regarding each exercise as if it were a small piece of art. For instance, lifting the arm up and down must not be done superficially. No. It must be done as a little tiny performance. While we are exercising we are trying to fuse the psychology of a creative person with the exercise, so that that exercise will not be somewhere else and we, as creative persons, be here. The exercise must be where our creative spirit is. These two conditions are very important if one wants to exercise in our way. Each time with a fresh approach, and to do it so that each small thing is an accomplished piece of art.

ATMOSPHERE

We have spoken about atmospheres, and how we must imagine the air filled with the atmosphere chosen for the exercise, then we start to move and speak with the aim that everything we do will be more and more in harmony with the imaginary air around us. That is the spine of the exercise on atmospheres. A certain creative power and will is awakened by this exercise for atmosphere.

CONCENTRATION

Concentration for us means to choose an object, either physical, audible, or imaginary, and try to merge with it more and more by going out of oneself to catch, to embrace, to grasp, to hold, to possess and then to merge with the object and become one with it. That is the spine of the exercise of concentration. Just as one can think either chaotically or in an organized way, just so the exercises on atmosphere or concentration can be done.

IMAGINATION

The best way to exercise the imagination is in three different degrees. 1) Try to imagine things which we know exist—something in our room. As if to remember the object, this is the first step to the imagination. 2) The next step is to imagine things which we have never seen, but have heard about. Here we have to imagine not only by means of remembering but by means of a certain activity which will shape for us certain things which we have heard about but which we do not know. 3) The third step is to imagine things which do not exist at all. Pure fantasy. Whether it is a character which we have never seen, or a plant, or a super-human being, but something which you cannot think of because you have never seen or heard of it. These three stages are sufficient for the moment: 1) The real thing which is not seen at the moment, but is remembered. 2) Something real which is half-known. 3) Something which is unknown—pure creation.

FEELING OF EASE

The best way to start these exercises is to recall your state of mind when you are in a sad, heavy mood, and compare it with moments when you are gay and happy. Pay attention to how differently you experience your own body in these two extreme moods. When you are gay, you feel your body almost without weight, and when you are in a heavy, depressed mood, you feel the weight of your body to be very heavy. By this means you can distinguish between the extremes. Then start to move and try to develop the feeling of ease.

Try to speak and let the words fly out of your speech apparatus more easily, regardless of the content. "How" it is said is important, because this "how" is actually the feeling of ease. The content can be very heavy, but the means of expression, the "how," that is the feeling of ease.

SUSTAINING

The "trick" of preparation or anticipation, movement or speech, and the sustaining—for this we must have the inner impulse, then the word or action, then the sustaining. While exercising this, it is very good to use our arms and hands, because this will give us a real impulse later on. Later we will talk about our psychology and its connection with our movements. Instead of exploring the part philosophically or psychologically, and then plunging into the part, knowing much about it but not being able to say one word, we have means of doing the same work, but starting with our actor's means of *exploring the part.*

THE OBJECTIVE

To exercise the objective means to choose the aim, and to imagine it as if already fulfilled.

CONTRASTS

There is another means for making our acting on the stage more expressive. The principle is a very simple one. Each time we have a part, or even parts, on which we have been working for several months—these are very suitable material—we must try to find, wherever we can, the contrasts in the part. Contrasts in every sense. For instance, I will give you some different examples to show that contrasts can be found everywhere. Let us take two sentences as an example: "Do you want me to go with you?" and "I will not go with you." These can be spoken in exactly the same way, and it will be one straight line, which means in every form of art that it is the poorest, weakest, most obvious expression.

The straight line is nothing for us—art requires curves, and spirals and such forms, but not the straight line, unless the straight line is used consciously in the psychology, the voice, etc., then, of course, it becomes a very strong means of expression. But if used throughout the whole performance, then it is a very dull business. The last time we exercised our scene it was a very straight line—noise, shouting, a straight line from the very beginning. Instead of which we must try to find many contrasts, many polar things which are everywhere.

For instance, you can speak the first sentence in a very quick tempo and the second sentence in a slow tempo—immediately there is something expressive there—or try it just the opposite. The contrast even in tempo makes it more expressive. You can combine these contrasts by speaking one sentence in a quick tempo and a low voice, or in a slow tempo and a loud voice. You can give one sentence a warm quality and the other a cold quality. You can play with the two sentences just as a juggler does, and actually that gives a great pleasure not only for you but for the audience. They cannot tolerate a straight line too long, but if there is a variety of polar things the audience will be absolutely with the actor.

You can do this with sentences, with scenes, with everything. For instance, let us take the Cellar scene and the Letter scene in *Twelfth Night*, in which the same characters meet twice. It is very helpful for the director to find such contrasts. The Cellar scene can be base and heavy, muted, pleasure in all physcial things such as eating, drinking, embracing, etc. And the Letter scene, or Garden scene, can be absolutely the opposite—everything unreal, like magic, not of this earth. Immediately the whole play gets relief.

It depends on the part, and the actor must know what he wants to do with the part. For instance, let us take the following contrasts from *King Lear*. The three speeches are from the one scene—the Heath scene. The first speech is, "Blow, winds, and crack your cheeks!," the second speech is, "Poor, naked wretches," and the third speech is, "Why, thou wer't better in thy grave than to answer with thine uncovered body this extremity of the skies."

It would be a good exercise for the actor to find what contrasts can be used in these three speeches. For instance, the "Blow, winds," speech can be spoken out of the will. Then the "Poor, naked wretches" speech can be spoken out of the region of the heart—it comes from the heart, and the "Why, thou wer't better in thy grave. . . ," can be from the head—thinking. So the same character can use the contrast of these three regions of will, feelings, and thought which we have spoken about. Lear will be more expressive if he uses such contrasts.

Then the director can imagine the play, and find the contrast between the beginning and the end. This can be found in every play, but we will take again the example of *King Lear*. It begins in a stately, abstract atmosphere in which everything is centered on a despotic being, who plays with people as with puppets. A depressed, heavy, hopeless atmosphere of unreal activity, as it were. The end is a catharsis—everything is the opposite from the beginning—if the beginning was heavy, the end must be as light as air. If at the beginning, Lear was opppressing everyone, in the end he is the victim of his destiny. In the beginning he was evil, and at the end he is enlightened. In the beginning he was sitting higher than all the others, and at the end he must die being down.

Everything must be used for expressing such contrasts. This will mold the characters, and then the characters can speak more staccato or, again, more legato, or at one moment warm and at another cold, or muted and open. Innumerable possibilities of contrasts are everywhere, and then the play will be much more expressive than it would be without such contrasts.

QUESTIONS AND ANSWERS

I was wondering about our last improvisation, based on atmosphere. Did you intend us to use actions, and have objectives which we chose for ourselves, or did you intend us to rely entirely on the atmospheres for our improvisation?

FOUR STAGES OF THE CREATIVE PROCESS

I intended the latter. Of course, we cannot switch off all our experience as actors, but for our present aims it would be better to concentrate just on the atmosphere, and see what will come out of it. What was wrong was that the atmosphere was forgotten and you started to act, because you are actors. It cannot be overcome immediately, but we must make the effort again and again to drop the things we have become accustomed to, when we are exercising new things. I should have made it clearer to you that the basis for the improvisation was *only* the atmosphere—*the four stages of the creative process:* 1) *atmosphere.* 2) *imagination.* 3) *incorporation.* 4) *inspiration.* Of course it takes tremendous courage to say "No" to all the things which you have been accustomed to using, but this courage must be found.

In what way would it have been different if we had all been aware of the atmosphere? Also, if we were not as aware as we were meant to be, would we just become aware of the atmosphere, and stop all the impulses to act? Would that be the final objective?

If we could stop all the old habits, other impulses would come which are much more subtle, much finer, more your own, more individual, more personal, because the things which you did, instead of the atmosphere, were very much "in general." Everyone can shout, everyone can go on like that, but what we are trying to do is to let the *individuality* come out and sparkle. It can be done only if we discard all our habits, and let our individualities respond to whatever we choose—in this instance it was the atmosphere. Then you will see that you are not poorer but actually much richer and more expressive as actors. You will see that nothing will be lost, if you will somehow switch off your old habits.

What you say about allowing finer, more individual things to come out of me is very appealing, but I don't understand how I can do it. In the improvisation for atmosphere the other day, I found myself involved with a lot of things. So much started to happen that I could not control, in your sense. What is the alternative to that? Must I sit back and wait for something to come?

I understand your question. We must not sit back and wait—that is fear which chokes us. First of all, because you are an actor you cannot sit and wait, except if you are embarrassed, then, of course, nothing happens. For example, let us take the moment when the sailors are drinking and talking to each other in the atmosphere, there is so much to do! Even the drinking alone in this atmosphere would be enough. As soon as you drink one imaginary glass in this atmosphere, you will be overwhelmed by the actions which come as a result.

Then what happens when we have to develop and continue the problem of the plot? Something is supposed to develop, and I am supposed to take part in it. When I am taking part in it, I lose some of the atmosphere. How much time should we allow ourselves to sit in the atmosphere, before we begin to be involved in the plot?

If we were going to rehearse a play, it would be a different thing. But I have chosen this improvisation as an example by which I can show you what I mean by the method—certain principles, methods, and "tricks." Therefore, it was not a normal rehearsal. A rehearsal would be quite a different thing, and this is only an attempt on my part to make my method as clear as possible, by means of acting in this improvisation. If it is not successful we do not need to worry about it, because certain understanding of the method will come, and that is my task.

May I say then that in the next improvisation I shall make it my task to wait to be pushed, rather than to get in there and push someone else.

If we go on with the atmospheres, then it would be very good, but I had hoped to take another step today, by giving you some lines for the improvisation. However, on principle, you are right. It would be better to wait and "listen" to the atmosphere. For instance, if you drink a glass of wine, having developed the atmosphere, there is no time needed to get the atmosphere—it will come immediately. As soon as you know that the atmosphere is one of drunken gaiety, then you do not need any time to wait because it is around you immediately, and you only have to know it.

I think the only way we know whether we are right or wrong is by criticism from you. You are the only one who can tell us whether we have understood your example.

I have never worked in terms of atmosphere before, but everything that happened in the improvisation has happened to me before. We feel impelled to do a lot of action. When the improvisation goes wrong, I think it should be stopped, and we should be told where we have gone off the track.

My fear was only that my criticism might be considered a destructive one, but if you will accept it as constructive, then I will do it.

Even after all this discussion I don't know whether I create the right atmosphere or not, or whether I was creating at all.

The main mistake last time was that, as modern actors, we are very easily led by action on the stage, and, first of all, by what we are doing and speaking. Therefore, we were immediately enticed into doing things instead of relying on this new element of atmosphere which would entice us to do and to speak, but in a different way. So there comes the question of "how" we act and speak with the atmosphere or without it, because the atmosphere is actually "how" things happens on the stage.

We can get up and drink a glass of wine, without atmosphere, but if we want to do it differently—that is "how"—we must find the atmosphere in which we are doing it. We change the atmosphere, not the action—the "how" will depend on different atmospheres. So this is the question of adding to the "what," the action, the "how" or the way I am doing it. And this "how" depends on the atmosphere and other things. Therefore, there is no question of whether you have created right or wrong atmospheres. You can change the atmosphere while you are acting, but the atmosphere must be there. There is only the question of whether you have lost the atmosphere, or whether you are still in it, doing and speaking things through the atmosphere, because of it, in it.

Is it true that when we are working properly with the atmosphere, it is something which we are giving back and forth. If you share something, you would not be working alone, but you would be absorbing what is created there.

Absolutely.

I feel the only time we got anywhere near the atmosphere was when we united in singing a song. Was that right or wrong?

When I say that the atmosphere was gone, that is not quite correct, because it was there in spite of certain wrong things. So I would say that not only was the song atmosphere there, but all the other atmospheres, too, however, they were not strong enough for us to get inspiration from them. So it is a question of balance.

We may understand atmosphere, but when we start to act, our old habits overwhelm the atmosphere. Therefore, without exercising this new thing, it is actually impossible to produce it. In time, it will become more and more obvious that atmosphere is one of the ways—one of the most important ways—to get new things out of ourselves, and to be original and ingenious each time. We do not have it because of many habits and clichés, which do not allow us to break through these things and create new things. It is a matter of having the courage to say "No" to these other things which are deceiving us.

Let us try to investigate and rely upon this atmosphere, by saying one sentence and doing a definite gesture which I will give you. Speak the sentence, "I love you," with this gesture, in the atmosphere of secrecy, very warm but very cautious.

Because you recognized that it was simple, your creative impulses were immediately there, and it was all much more individual than in the noisy exercise you did the other day. But whether it is Hamlet or some uncomplicated thing, it is just the same thing if we have this simple technique.

It was easier for me because I was all alone, but the disturbing thing is to do it when you have to work with so many people. How do you keep in the atmosphere, if your partner is not in it?

The difficulty of our art is that in general we depend so much on other people. This problem has to be solved by a similar culture, if we are aiming at the same thing and have the same training; then it will be diminished and the problem will disappear.

If I am working in a Broadway play, and am the only actor who knows the method, is there any way I can lead my partners?

To a certain extent you cannot, but many things can be done. If you cannot entice everyone, some of them will follow you, and you can accomplish many things, being alone. Of course, it is difficult, and it is one of the unhappy things in our modern theatre.

ACTORS AND THE METHOD

I have tried certain things in Germany when I was acting with Reinhardt. German actors are incredible from the point of view of clichés . . . like rocks and stones. Do you think that a group of German actors would come together as we have? They would not even dare to ask anyone what they thought of this or that. It is such a polite country, in the wrong sense of the word. Nobody had any interest for what I was doing, but I used one thing, although I knew it would be taking a risk. While the other actor was speaking certain words, I did certain things by which the audience's attention was directed to me. The poor actor was very unhappy but he could not find the person who was doing it. Finally, when he discovered that it was I, he came to me, pale and trembling. He begged me to allow him to act alone, instead of trying to find out what I was doing so that together we could try to do something more interesting. But he would never allow that. Another time, I changed the *mise en scene* while acting, and the stage manager whispered, "Stop it! You will be fined for this!" When I asked what was wrong, he said, "You have changed your *mise en scene*, and what will the others do?" It was very difficult to act in Germany—they are so stiff there—like a corset.

CROWD SCENE PSYCHOLOGY

We often make another little mistake—and this you have done in the improvisation the other day. When there is a crowd scene actors make one mistake—suddenly they forget that they are individuals, and each one tries to become a crowd. They try to perform the whole scene, all the noises, etc., instead of waiting for the result, because crowd scenes are always the result of many things going on. But actors confuse this, and each one tries to act the whole crowd. If you will try to remain individuals in this crowd scene, you will get a very attractive scene.

APPROACH TO THE REHEARSAL

The first thing we have tried to apply was the atmosphere. The second thing was the imagination, and I have suggested that you read the text of a play, not so much for the content, which will happen of itself, but to imagine while the words are spoken—see and hear them and see how the action goes on in your imagination while you are reading the text. In this way you will get the text through the imagination and not through the content.

After the first draft of the performance is clear enough in your imagination, then the next step will be to incorporate this imagination. Whether right or wrong. Rehearsals are for the aim of finding better things. First imagine the whole thing, imagine the atmosphere, imagine the characters, imagine how the words are spoken. It is always important to be able to create one image, we can also create another and a better one. Read the play by imagining it.

QUALITIES OR CONTRASTS

Let us try to enumerate the things which we see in this room. Try to enumerate them in one long, straight line of speech. Now start by speaking slowly, and then increase the tempo. At once it becomes more expressive. It becomes some psychological thing at the end. Or try the opposite—nothing will come of it if it is even, equal, or straight. Of course, it can be made consciously even, but then it must be used very consciously. Let us speak equally, then more and more slowly. From this you will see that we can combine many qualities.

First speak with the quality of being annoyed, then become more and more interested in the things you are looking at. Begin quickly and then become slower; it is immediately interesting to watch, and that is acting. Simply the process of expressing is interesting. Such acting is more interesting possibly than *Hamlet* often is. If we can do such things in this simple exercise, how wonderful it would be to do such things with Shakespeare, whose plays are full of these contrasts. Let us repeat the exercise, first it is quick, annoyed, and loud, then at the end slow, interested, and soft.

These qualities or contrasts will entice certain feelings in us. For instance, if we imagine that our individuality is longing to express itself, but the means which we place at its disposal are so even, so uninteresting, that the individuality cannot use them. Let us imagine that this straight line is nothing that the individuality can use, but as soon as we give a little contrast, such as quick and slow, the individuality immediately tries to use it. A little exercise will give us ourselves, and will enrich us by means of ourselves, because we have everything in us as actors.

EXERCISE

By taking a position and holding the hand, say "Please don't." Then place the other hand on the chest and again say "Please don't." Another nuance will come. That is pure acting—no philosophy, no psychology behind it. We move in a certain way and that awakens our emotional life. Now add the fourth movement—drop the hands to the side and say "Please don't." Don't think of it consecutively—just go on and see what happens.

This is the proof that our actor's nature does not want to stop. If we have injected our being with something—objective, atmosphere, or simply gesture, it must go on and that is acting. That is improvisation which must always be present on the stage. It is clichés which make us dead and which stop us.

IMAGINATION

One more suggestion: I have already suggested that we make exercises in several ways—1) By seeing something in my imagination which I know exists, but which I cannot see with my physical eyes. 2) To imagine things which I have never seen but which I know about. 3) To create something which is absolutely the product of pure fantasy.

Now I suggest another exercise which is a guide to imagining the character, which you will choose or create anew. Try to imagine this character fulfilling objectives, different objectives—purely in the imagination. Ask the character to fulfill the objective, "I want to get some money." Imagine some situation—where the character is, and from whom he or she wants to get the money. Try to imagine the character fulfilling the objective. That will be the next step. Follow your imagination so that there will be no breaks in it.

FEELING OF EASE

Recall a moment when you were gay and happy. What was the weight of your body? Now lift your arms and hands, making the movement a little piece of art. Now toss the imaginary ball from one to the other, using the body very freely, everyone taking part all the time. Then we will begin to feel something flowing in our bodies. So many emotions will come to us, if we take full part in this. Everything immediately appeals to the feelings, which shows what a childlike nature the artist has, if we appeal to it. This feeling of ease is one of the four qualities which the actor must have at his disposal all the time.

Sixth Class

The Creative Process:
The Inspiration—The Method

November 24, 1941

When scientists today try to calculate the ability of the human heart to pump so much liquid which moves through the big and small channels of the body, they cannot see that it is mechanically impossible to imagine such a pump as our heart. First of all, the human heart, which would be able to move this quantity of blood, must be much bigger and stronger than it is, and the substance of the heart would have to be of quite different material. The whole secret is that the blood moves and the heart follows, but our physiologists are not so well developed in science that they can accept this. They don't think the blood can move of itself, but they believe that the heart moves of itself.

THE CREATIVE PROCESS AND THE INSPIRATION

It is just the same with the creative process and the inspiration. It was once true that the creative process and the inspiration came of themselves, but now it is no longer so. Now we have to adjust our organism, physically and mentally, to the process of "in"spiration, and, therefore, the method is needed. A few decades ago, if you suggested to a gifted actor that he study a method, he would tell you that he did not need it because he had inspiration. But living in our present modern life, to cling to the old belief that inspiration comes of itself would be wrong. One of our enemies is the intellect, and the other is not know-ing that the technique or method is needed, and this is often the most detrimental thing for us. Because if we deny the method, we cannot assume it, and if we do not know it exists, we cannot assume it either.

THE METHOD

When we look upon this point which we call the creative process and the inspiration, it is, of course, our last and only aim, and we must look upon this point as though it were the center, and on the periphery there are so many doors through which we had to look. By looking through these doors at the moment of inspiration, what will we get at the end? We will get only the method. When we speak about the atmosphere, it is one of the doors which we can open and see there is the creative process, and there is the spark of inspiration. We open another door, which may be the feeling of ease perhaps, then the door of the imagination—all the points of our method are these doors.

How does one reach the state where it is necessary to look through all these doors? It is a very painful experience which we all have. This necessity, this painful necessity, is there in every one of us to some extent. We know, we feel, we experience that as actors, as artists, as creators, as human beings we are rich in and full of unfulfilled desires, undiscovered thoughts, unexperienced feelings, all of which are looming somewhere before us.

In our everyday life certain intimations of ourselves we can have, although if we were inwardly free, we might live quite a different life, speak quite differently, react to life quite differently. But now try to look at what we are doing on the stage, quite objectively and without self pity. We are psychologically crippled beings—we are so small and narrow-minded while we are representing this or that character. We are almost puppets—if we have, let us say, six feelings in our life—schematically speaking—we bring one of them to the stage. If we have six thoughts in life, we show one of them from the stage, instead of becoming, during the creative process on the stage, enlarged, enriched, spreading beings fulfilling all our creative desires and emotions.

We could free ourselves on the stage and satisfy not only ourselves but the audience also, because they are in the same position—they live lives which are regulated by the clock and they have no real imagination or freedom. On the stage we can find that all the moments can be filled with the most profound, the utmost inner things which we bear in ourselves, but which we cannot experience or express during our everyday life.

Instead of which we become smaller and smaller. For instance, let us take the characters of Hamlet, Ophelia, or Cordelia, they can be for us wide open doors through which we find ourselves, instead of which we become smaller than they and even smaller than we are in everyday life, because if there is no moment of inspiration, no signpost leading to the inspiration, then we are doomed to a crippled existence on the stage.

When one feels he cannot display himself on the stage, then the torture begins, because one feels he is sitting in a psychological prison. Then the necessity arises to see the creative process from all possible doors. So we know that the method has a number of points of view on the creative process, and that the necessity for this method is because of the painful experience of not being able to live our life fully enough on the stage, but on the contrary becoming smaller and more contracted.

OUTER EVENTS AND THE INNER LIFE

We have spoken about the four stages of the creative process, and have illustrated them with a series of charts. Now let us look at the creative process from another point of view. Let us describe it differently. What aspect of the creative process would allow us to live this full life? Imagine that there are two possibilities—one is ourselves and the richness which we cannot discover, and another is the wrong kind of play lying there before us. When we modern actors don't know or don't want to know what the creative process is, we do the following thing. We take this wrong kind of play, and instinctively close ourselves and say, "Now I am alone, and I won't show anything of myself, because if I do, I will immediately be out of the style of the present theatre. I have to show my clichés, but not myself, because it is so embarrassing to show myself on the stage."

So I close myself and take the play which is all outside, all external, and I begin to study the text and then, by means of clichés, I begin to try to pronounce the words from the stage. The play remains an outer thing, and the inner part of me remains inner and still more closed. An illusion takes place—a phantom consisting of certain clichés comes out of me, takes hold of me and speaks the words with a dead voice. The play is finished, the phantom has done its work, and I can go home.

But the right way would be to take this wrong play, and turn it into my inner life so that it will become a symbol for my inner new life, which I have to discover within me. It will not be the wrong play then, but will be me expressing myself through the suggestions given by the author. So the outer thing becomes the inner thing, and my inner life becomes an outer thing. I give it to my audience, and I do not keep it inside me. If we try to look upon all the points of our method, we will see that they are the means of changing our inner life into an outer one. If this idea becomes a living thing in one's mind, it means not only to have the picture.

I must tell you certain ideas and conceptions, if you are to understand my aim. All the points of the method can be understood from the point of view of transforming the outer thing into the inner life, and changing the inner life into the outer event. To know this means to be able, to a great extent, to manage it and to do it. Leo Tolstoy once said that if you are angry and want to be revenged on someone, instead of trying to preach a moral to oneself you should imagine very concretely, day after day, that you have got the opportunity to revenge yourself, and that your victim is down. The more you realize that you are victorious and your victim is crushed, the more surely this knowledge will bring you the fruit which you don't expect. It is your real desire. You will lose the desire to be revenged, and you will have such compassion for your victim, and the real true man in you will show because you will know what you are aiming at.

If we know what we are aiming at in the method, we will get it, not only as I suggest it, but you will get it for yourself. Each one of us is a creative individual, and before he gets the method personally he must imagine himself developed by means of the method. It has to be your method. You have to conceive of it in quite a different way, and no one else can conceive of it in the same way. I must give you my conception of the method, and you must imagine how you will accept it. Then you will get a vision of the method which is yours and not mine, and you can develop it according to your own individuality. If you think I am going to impose something on you, you will throw it away. The point is to individualize the things which I am going to tell you.

Now let us take one more point from our method. I have told you that there are four qualities which each actor must have as permanent qualities which he can apply whenever his creative individuality wants to apply them, and in which way. One of them was the *feeling of ease*, and another was the *feeling of form*.

FEELING OF FORM—THE ACTOR'S BODY

The feeling of form which I have in mind is, of course, the outer form starting with our body—we must try to meditate upon our own body as a form, to experience it as a form. We forget things which we have no right to forget. We have to realize certain facts which are so obvious, so well-known to everyone that no one thinks about them any more. But we must know that our body is a form—a definite, concrete form.

At first, it may seem difficult to realize that we have arms and hands which are able to move in different directions. It is so obvious, therefore, our movements are formless and shapeless, unless we go through this obvious thing consciously. If we try to realize that we have arms, hands, legs, and feet, and are astonished by the fact, then we will become able to manage them subconsciously with much more expressiveness.

Decades ago, people were much less poisoned by the intellect—their lives were not like ours, torn to pieces by everything around us, radio, television, telephone—senseless distractions, but we have grown accustomed to them. In the past, people were much freer in their spirits and souls, their nerves were much more sound, their heart-beats more normal, their breathing much deeper than ours and many, many physical and psychological things were not lying upon them like a terrible weight, which lies upon us even though we may not feel it.

When we awaken again this feeling of our bodies as a form, it will give us a

new and definite ability to manage and govern our bodies in the most expressive way, and more than that, we will be able to get inspiration from our
bodies.

Here I must again speak about a small point—we get inspirations from our
bodies although we do not know it, but our bodies inspire us mostly in a
wrong, narrow way because they are the expression of certain ideas we have
about ourselves. If I am fat and have a big tummy, then I express a certain idea.
If I am very thin and have a very thin waist, I cannot get rid of this idea and all
my inspirations come from this thin waist. Or I have a well-developed chest,
which gives another psychology. If, for instance, a very fat person says, "I will
run and bring it to you," of course there is something humorous about it.

Therefore, there is something which comes purely from our bodies as a form,
which inspires us consciously or subconsciously. If our bodies are developed to
such an extent that it will be just the same which waist, which shoulders, which
feet we have, if we are able to manage our bodies to such an extent that we will
get inspiration from the *whole* body, then we will get inspiration from our
physical bodies. It may sound strange that something like inspiration, which is
very spiritual, can help us in this way, but it is true. So this suggestion to experience the body as a form is again the way to the same point—to the creative
process and the inspiration.

EXERCISE

The simpler we do this exercise the better. First try to realize, each for himself,
that you have a body which is upright. No other being in the world has such a
position—animals are horizontal and even apes are bound to the earth in an
ugly way. So realize that you are upright. Then realize that your head is like a
crown on this part of your being, and that your head is round. This is the only
round part of your body. Then realize that you touch the earth but you do not
belong to it. Now recall that animals are bound to the earth with all four legs.
The cow, for instance, is completely bound to the earth. But we can touch the
earth here, there, and everywhere. Now move about and realize that you are
touching the earth by pushing it back. Then realize the following fact: that the
animal has to use all of its four extremities. Now take a position and realize that
being an animal you cannot move your hands and arms. What a terrible thing
that is. How can you express yourself? Even the head is turned to the earth.

Compare this imaginary animal psychology with your ability to stand
upright and have free hands and arms. We must appreciate the fact that they
are free. Now you will see that the arms and hands are the most expressive part
of our physical being. But we confuse two things, we confuse our heads
—including all the most subtle muscles of the face—with our arms and hands
and try to express things by making gestures with our faces. That is a terrible
thing. When we laugh on the stage, for instance, and try to show the teeth,

etc.—all such grimaces are made because we confuse the movement of the hands and arms, and substitute movements of the face. All such grimaces are coming from our subconscious confusion because we do not know what our arms and hands are for. When we keep them in our pockets, there is nothing for us to do but make faces. When we learn to use our arms and hands, then our eyes will become more expressive on the stage, and that is right because our whole life will be concentrated in our eyes. We have the right to radiate with our eyes.

It is sometimes considered that moving the hands and arms is a national instinct—for instance, Russian, Italian, and French people move the arms and hands too freely for American taste. Your taste will tell you how much you should use this ability. The ability must be there, but how to apply it is a question which you, as an individual artist, must find out. But what is wrong—whether you are American or foreign—is to always have the hands in your pockets.

After we realize that this round thing, our head, must not produce gestures or grimaces, and after we realize that we have our arms and hands free from the earth, and that we are upright and touch the earth by pushing it back, then we have to realize one more thing in order to experience our body as a form, and that is that we have in our chests an imaginary center, then we shall find that all our movements on the stage, and in life, will become much freer and richer and more expressive. If we are not dragging ourselves behind us, which is always the case when we do not know where our center is. When I know where I am centralized as a form, then I move forward, being led by this center. The whole harmonious psychological attitude is there for every one of us, and this is the key to many abilities.

To feel oneself harmonious inwardly means that one is able to produce inharmonious things much freer and better. On the other hand, if we are always inharmonious and try to produce beautiful things, we are always wrong. Now walk around being led by this center. Feel the center in your chest, and see how the whole body will become grateful to you for harmonizing it, so that the arms and hands and legs and feet are somehow in their right place, as it were.

You will find that both physical and psychological balance will come, and the body which has been made harmonious gives us inspiration. The scope of the inspiration is wider, the ideas which the artist and actor will get will be much richer and more interesting, if they come from a sound, harmonized body.

We can recall again the fat person who tries to run for something, if we penetrate into his imagination and see how he thinks of himself, that is quite a different world. It is a very different kind of thing from that of another person with another kind of body. His world is different from the world of any one of us. A tall person has, of course, a different kind of imagination from that of a short person, but the only way is to harmonize our own body, and then be able to imagine oneself fat, tall, short, or thin.

Of course, the physically fat person cannot imagine and perform a thin person, but if he tries to harmonize his body in the way we are speaking about, he can give the impression of a thin person. Pickwick was like that, I imagine, because his character was somehow organized, but Falstaff was quite different because his whole psychology was around his stomach and even lower. Sir Andrew Aguecheek's center was in his nose.

CHARACTERIZATION

We will touch upon another point in our method; that of characterization. We must have the psychology of an ideal body, even if we do not have a physical one, then we will see how easy and pleasant it will be to imagine and perform any bodily characterization. Very humorous things can be found in this way. For instance, if you will imagine that your whole center is in your nose, or your center is behind you, a fat, heavy, round thing which drags you back. Your whole body will become expressive through your inner imaginary body.

Now walk around to the rhythm of a march, recalling all the things we have mentioned—the head a round form, the center in the chest, the arms, and legs starting from the center like a big scissors.

MOVEMENT AS FORM

The next point is that we must experience the movement as form itself. This is also very important. Because if we develop this ability to experience our movements as forms, then again we shall become more expressive, even if our hands and arms are in our pockets! If you do it with a feeling of form, then it means something. For this exercise, try to stretch your right arm out and experience the process as a form. You begin and you stop, and what happens is the form in movement. When we experience this feeling we will know what it means to experience form in movement.

Now get up and experience the movement as a form which you carve and mold in the air around you. Now sit down with the same feeling of form. Do it pedantically so that later on it will become free, spontaneous and subconscious. Then combine movements of your arms and hands when standing up, and take a few steps forward. Do not drop the movement vaguely or accidentally, but decide when you are going to stop the exercise. You may become a little stiff and staccato in your movements at first, but it will pass. Now take a certain position and imagine that it is in the air, then move away from it and imagine that the form remains in the air. This will awaken the feeling of form in you.

Now shake hands with the feeling of form, and say "Hello" or "Goodbye." Now three persons will meet and improvise the meeting each time, by adjusting to each other. You must experience the feeling of form of three persons meeting. You will see that your actor's nature becomes more and more satisfied as you do the exercises.

Now let us experience some abstract movements. One person will take a position and hold it, and another person will join him and take a position in harmony with the other. Now another step. We must combine the feeling of form, plus the theme which will be given music in this case. We will listen to the music and, feeling the theme intuitively, we will take positions in harmony with the musical theme and the bodily positions which are creating and expressing it. Now let us take a theme such as jealousy.

FEELING OF EASE

Let us once more exercise the feeling of ease in the simplest way by raising our arms and hands, which are the most expressive things in our actor's profession. Now take a chair and move it with the feeling of ease. It will lose its weight because we are filled with the feeling of ease. Now the whole group will take the heavy table with the feeling of ease, and lift it so that the table will seem to be without weight. Now each member of the group will get up and say "Hello" to the whole group—it will be a little performance for each one, again using the feeling of ease. It is good when rehearsing sometimes to drop everything and just take a feeling of ease.

Seventh Class

Feeling of the Whole

November 28, 1941

If the actor will read the script in his imagination often enough, he will come to the rehearsal with many new things. Now let us read the text of our scene out loud. While reading the text, rely upon the atmosphere, and imagine how you would act, but don't actually do it. The first atmosphere is chaotic and wild without any reason.

SETTINGS—*MISE EN SCENE*

The setting for the play very often remains absolutely abstract to the actors, because of the mistaken idea that our profession is somehow one of floundering. It is a very pleasant thing to know the setting as well as one knows one's own room. Therefore, we have to become familiar with the setting by, first of all, putting some questions to ourselves. Where are the lights, for instance? You must have in mind the atmosphere when you decide such things. We must develop a sense for these things. It is not just the same thing wherever the lights are. Again, when the director fixes the *mise en scene*, it is only good when the actors are free to improvise while the director is giving certain *mise en scene*. Try to understand how our scene can look: 1) Chaotic. 2) Unified by the song. 3) Intimate.

Now take the first cues. Those who speak the lines are already on stage and the others are coming on. Those on stage must speak so that everyone will hear, and the task of the others is to speak as if in chaos, but so as not to distract from the others. All the characters who are not speaking are moving around in a restless way.

To recapitulate the first steps toward producing the play: 1) The setting must be well-known to the actor in every way. 2) Find first the main atmospheres—in the imagination, and then by concrete improvising under the suggestions of the director. When the first atmospheres are there, with the special *mise en scene*, then it is the basis on which the director can direct, and the actors can act with mutual understanding. Then the director will not be a despot, and the actors his slaves. The actors will understand the director's slightest suggestion, because it will come out of this understanding.

FEELING OF THE WHOLE

I have said that there are three qualities which the actor must have as continuous abilities. One is the feeling of ease, another the feeling of form, and the third one we may call the feeling of the whole. The actor must have this ability to grasp the play as a whole, and inside are little "wholes." If there is a word which is of special significance, the actor has to have the ability to grasp this word as one whole thing.

This special ability to grasp things in time and space as one whole thing is important from many points of view. First, if this ability is developed, the actor will not be lost among the many details, but they will become organic parts of the whole. We often see actors who are able to act so that there is a marvelous series of details, but it is still not pleasant to look at because the actor has not the ability to grasp the whole thing, inside of which will be elaborated the "embroidery."

This feeling of the whole, which is a very pleasant one, can be developed slowly by very simple means. Let us do again the movement of lifting your arms and hands up and down, with the aim of experiencing this simple thing as one whole complete thing. It is a purely psychological thing. A psychological thing with which you can grasp everything. This beautiful feeling of "*one*" thing must be awakened. If you will awaken this feeling, you will even dream about "one"—it is so complete and beautiful.

Now do the exercise twice with your arms, then next to it once and then pause, and then bring the arms down and make it one whole thing. Whatever may be the complicated tasks or business between partners, if you have this feeling of the whole it will suggest the most correct timing. It is the best inspiration for many things—rhythm, timing, meaning—all will become clear.

PREPARATION AND SUSTAINING

Exercise

Sit down, get up, change your place and then sit down again, and experience it as a whole. You will meet many disturbing things, but try to overcome them with this feeling of the "one" thing.

Exercise

Ask your partner what time it is; the partner gives the answer, but both must have the feeling of the whole.

Now you will see that this feeling of the whole is impossible without *preparation* and *sustaining*, and it becomes so pleasant for us and for the audience. These inner things which we cannot show but can experience, that is what the audience wants and needs.

Now repeat the exercise of asking someone for the time, but both must experience the preparation and sustaining together. This is a fine mutual business. Now experience two different things as two waves, but still one thing. First the preparation, then ask the question, "What time is it?", then sustain. Then begin another wave by saying, "Let's go," then go and sustain. All one thing.

ENSEMBLE OR CONTACT

We use the feeling of the whole mostly with our partners on the stage, so it requires a very fine mutual understanding and sensitiveness to our partners. There are other exercises which prepare us for this fine ensemble feeling, or contact.

Exercise

Sit in a circle so that you can see each other. In order to be sensitive to one another, it is not enough just to see or hear the other person. We must have another imaginary organ, and we must awaken it in ourselves. In this exercise we must all get up at the same time, without any agreement having been made among us.

OUTER AND INNER LEVELS OF ACTING

Listen and look at each other, and rely upon this third thing which is this *highly developed sensitiveness*. This is the thing which we are actually acting with, not only with our hands and voices, but with something more. This is one of the things which we have to develop. The world becomes bigger for us, and there are many new levels of acting, and the audience will be spellbound if there are at least two levels—one physical and outer and this other inner thing which we have just experienced.

Eighth Class

The Role of the Director

December 1, 1941

MEANS OF APPROACHING THE PLAY

To be able to go on with our sketch, we must investigate another point which will lead us to the next series of rehearsals. There is one very interesting process in human beings, and in actors especially, which can be used not only when we are preparing a part, but also by the director as well. It seems to me that it simplifies considerably the process of finding the part, on the one hand, and on the other how to convey to the actors the director's ideas without speaking or philosophizing too much.

This often takes place, and it was particularly true in the Moscow Art Theatre. We were sitting at the table for months and months, speaking about our parts and our characters, and becoming very clever and wise about the play, but none of us could begin to act! Then came the most difficult moment, the most difficult period, when we stopped talking and began to work, and we saw that nothing had come from all our analyzing of the part and the play. Our intellectual approach always killed the desire and ability to act until after several difficult days, when we remembered that we were actors.

But there is a means of approaching the play and the part without speaking too much. For the initial part of the work it is definitely good; I have tried it and it has been successful, but how long it can be preserved during the process of rehearsal is a different question. The point is the following one. We can easily imagine it by shutting one eye, as it were, but what shall we see? We will see that we are obliged to do two things on the stage, and these things include everything in the whole of acting. One thing is, we have always to *do* something, whether outwardly moving and speaking, or by having an objective, which means we are inwardly moving towards our aim. In either case, it is always a movement—either visible or invisible. The second part of this all-inclusive thing is how we do it. If we really try, in the initial period of our work, to grasp the part and the play from the point of view of "*what*" has been done, and "*how*" it has been done, then we have everything.

WILL, OR ACTION AND QUALITIES, OR FEELINGS

If, for instance, I ask you to take a chair and place it in a certain place, that is doing or "what" I am doing. Now the question remains, "how" do I do it? All the "how's" imaginable can be interpreted as qualities of my doing, of my acting. I can do it with the quality of "care"—and what is that if it is not acting? Simple, but complete acting. I am *doing* something with a certain *quality*. You may say to yourself, for instance, no feelings, no philosophy, no psychology or anything of that sort, only the chosen business with the chosen qualities. The result will be that you will awaken the most precious thing in the actor's profession—your feelings. You cannot move the chair with the quality of "care" without awakening something inside you. You can do everything, with all qualities. Whatever name you care to give it, it can become a quality. This is an important key to acting, and with it everything becomes simple.

Let us take the example of Hamlet and Horatio on the castle tower, waiting for the ghost to appear. What is Hamlet doing? He is projecting his attention in one way. He can project his being with the quality of "anxiety" and immediately there will be something—the first stone on which you can base other things. The director can tell you to combine two qualities—"anxiety" and "warmth," for instance. Everything becomes possible. You will come to more and more complicated things, and, from the actor's point of view, the part can be prepared very quickly as a result. But really prepared, and not empty clichés which are always following us.

Secondly, the simple action, and the simple quality will appeal to our utmost inner life, as we are not touching our feelings first, we are not tearing our soul to pieces to find our feelings, which cannot be found in that way. When the actor cannot find his feelings—for instance, tender love for a child—if he tells the director that he has never had a child, the director can answer him that everyone can give the quality of tenderness and love to his actions.

Simultaneously we take the action of moving the chair with the quality of "care." Neither is the result, they are only the springboard for awakening the two main things which actors must always use to the fullest extent—our will, or action, and our feelings. For action we must just choose *what* to do, or the *action*, and for the future feelings, we must choose *how* to do it, or the *quality*.

Suppose you choose one of Hamlet's soliloquies. Does the quality come from what you are doing?

It is one thing actually. What you are doing, and the quality with which you are doing it is actually one thing upon which you agree. The action never dictates the quality, nor the quality the action—it is a unit.

Let us take Hamlet's soliloquy: "But now I am alone." How he avenges his father's death is colored by certain feelings. His action is to avenge his father's death, but with certain qualities or "how's."

My aim was to simplify even the most complicated things, and, therefore, I have spoken about the action as a gesture.

In Juliet's speech, "Romeo, Romeo, wherefore art thou?", let us say her action is to pierce the distance, to find him, and her quality is one of "yearning." Would her action be to speak to someone with the quality of yearning, on top of which you would add all the other things?

Right. But now let us add something. If we describe what our action is, then we are describing our action by speaking about it. If the same is true with the qualities, then we are back with the Moscow Art Theatre and speaking without end! Therefore, the whole complicated business of Juliet is to be found out "gropingly," for which we don't need anything but the actor's talent. When the actor says, "I am groping," before she knows all the actions, then such complicated actions as Juliet's has to be simplified to the degree where the actor can show it, with simple physical gestures—with hands, arms, and body—then we are at the right point.

Nothing can be simpler or more appealing to us as actors. So Juliet in this moment is "groping," but with which quality? The quality of "longing." Now do the same gesture but with the quality of longing in your fingers, hands, arms, and body. When you have whatever psychology you choose, and you decide to turn it into a simple physical gesture with a certain quality, then you have the basis for developing your part, and for awakening your own emotional life and will impulses. Your creative imagination and everything will add to it until you become inspired, when everything goes, and you are simply acting.

ATMOSPHERE

I have wanted to ask you for some time about the question of atmosphere. I have seen very good actors led into a very bad thing—what I would call playing the mood, that is playing the result of the mood. For ten or twenty minutes we do not see what the actor is doing, we only see him sending out a certain mood. Many good actors are betrayed into this through a lack of action. How can that be avoided?

First of all, I must answer that in the whole method which we are exploring, you will not find a single place in which we appeal to feelings, because it is the most dangerous, treacherous point. As soon as we try to appeal to our feelings, we are out of control. We lose our action and flounder in the mood, and begin to lie more and more. All the points we have spoken of are only the ways to the feelings, but we never call directly on these feelings themselves. I have tried to explain that we have to imagine the atmosphere around us filled with certain things. That saves us from squeezing the feelings. For instance, if we imagine the air of a cathedral—the air filled with awe—of course our feelings will react to this.

I don't believe the atmosphere can be characterized. It comes from one's relationship to the object or person. For instance, the relationship of this class to Michael Chekhov is an atmosphere. That atmosphere has already changed, and my attitude became quite different to that of anybody else in the class—it became a personal thing, an individual thing.

In my opinion the atmosphere is the feeling one gets, which may be an entirely individual adjustment to, let us say, the moonlight, or the garden, the balcony, and so on. You don't have the same feeling as you would in the daylight on the beach. If you use the atmosphere with the action, then you can't be involved in a mood. You have your action which does not become static, and you are expressing yourself in action. For instance, each of us has a reaction to the night, but it is not the same.

I think we are confusing two things—acting, and our own personal feelings. If we are given a situation and an atmosphere, and we decide that we are going to work for an atmosphere of "awe," what I feel is not important; I only have to work for the atmosphere.

Does it mean that you should not have your individual reactions? Where is the difficulty?

What can we get from the generalized atmosphere, rather than from the particular character and his particular reactions? You say, for instance, that there is a general atmosphere of the tavern in the moonlight. What can we get from that which is different from the individual reaction?

The atmosphere, in the way that we have spoken of it, has to be imagined as a thing existing *objectively*. First of all, we must forget ourselves—whether we individually experience the awe of the cathedral or not is not important. The important thing is the imagination we have of the play in which this moment takes place. Different characters come into this cathedral—one experiences awe, another is indifferent, while the third becomes cynical, let us say. That is the theme of the play—a cynical character in the atmosphere of awe—otherwise the cynicism would not mean anything.

Does that not mean that you are taking a cliché when you say that the cathedral is awesome, or the moonlight romantic?

We can take many examples. If we have a cathedral on the stage, the atmosphere will depend upon the play, and what is going on. Remember *Murder in the Cathedral*, and it's atmosphere. I have used the cathedral, and the catastrophe on the street, simply as examples, but there are no clichés in our understanding of atmosphere. We must realize that whether we are trying to identify the atmosphere in everyday life or in a play, we must find it from the life situation or the play quite objectively.

Now let us imagine the cathedral with the atmosphere of awe. Whether I become cynical or full of awe, that is my personal business, but as soon as I act a part in a play in which the director wants the atmosphere of awe, I have to imagine it because I am taking part in the play. Even if I have the character of a cynic, I must still imagine it, because otherwise I do not know what to do in the play.

Does the actor have to create the atmosphere as any particular character?

Let us say that we have decided to create the atmosphere of awe which is written in the play. We have to do it by our means of imagining the air around us filled with the atmosphere. Then the feeling thing happens. The more you grow into your character, the more you react to this atmosphere as a character, and then we have just what the author wants. He combines so many characters in the one atmosphere of a scene, an act, or the whole play. But whether you, as a character, are cynical towards the atmosphere of awe, or are sympathetic to it, you must accept it, otherwise you will be out of the style of the play, or you will not belong to the scene.

Suppose you are a cynical character and the director has told you that the atmosphere is one of awe, what happens to your character?

I react as the character would react, but in order to react to something, there must be something to react upon. If there is no atmosphere of awe for me, because I am a cynical character, then I am not taking part in the play. I will tell you later what *the order of work* is.

Do you mean that the atmosphere is created by the play, and is the result of the play?

ORDER OF WORK:
ATMOSPHERE—GESTURE WITH
QUALITIES—CHARACTERIZATION

I would suggest that we drop the question of where the atmosphere comes from, because that will lead us to psychological analysis which will not be of any use to us. Your actor's intuition accepts, for instance, the atmosphere of a very dirty tavern in our scene. We have the means in our actors' souls to grasp intuitively the atmosphere, then we have the means to imagine this atmosphere around us, and that is all we need. Simultaneously we have to produce the gestures with qualities, and the characterization. *So we have the order:* 1) Atmosphere. 2) Gesture with qualities. 3) Characterization—and the whole composition is there in the simplest way.

Of course, there is an even simpler way, which is to use clichés but we deny this, because clichés close the actor's soul rather than open it. But to find the way to these vivid, alive and original things we have to do something—we have to sacrifice our energy.

There are two ways—one is a long one which was developed in the Moscow Art Theatre to the finest degree—that was analysis. Of course, they acted well in the long run, but this analysis was almost a disease. The other way is the one we are speaking about—to simplify things without losing anything. To make a gesture we use everything—our will. By applying the qualities we awaken our feelings. By creating the atmosphere, we envelope the play in one thing, which is the soul of the play, and by this we create a new, ingenious approach to the play. The actors will feel much freer to express themselves, than to be under the pressure of clichés, or to be pierced by intellectual speculations which are clever, but which are detrimental to acting.

The atmosphere is something which belongs more to the play or the scene, and the personal reaction of the character belongs to the character, so that the character reacting to the atmosphere is the character in the play. The character who does not create the atmosphere or react to it is a strange body in the play. For instance, let us say you must create the atmosphere of fear, and react to it personally. You may tell the director that you are fearless, and you have the right to say so as a private person when you are not acting, but since you are an actor—whether fearless or not as an individual—it has no connection with our profession. As actors, we have to create the fear around us, in order to be able to act the play. So at the same time that we are acting, we have to sacrifice our own personality.

TRANSFORMED FEELINGS

In this connection I mentioned something in our first talk, and I will now re-mind you of it. We might say that when we feel something on the stage it is our own feeling, and that no one gives it to us. But that is not quite so. Of course, we feel things, but there are two different realms in which there are two different kinds of feelings. In one realm there are the feelings which we awaken by the "death of the grandfather" which we have spoken about. The pain of your grandfather's death may be still fresh, but it is personal, and you cannot act it. Of course, it might help you if you were acting a sad part. But there is another realm of feelings which come from a certain subconscious realm of our life, and they have come through absolutely transformed.

Through our subconscious we have experienced all the feelings. So if we try to apply the fresh feeling which we are living with now, it could be dangerous even for our physical nerves. But if we apply the transformed feelings which have gone through a complicated process, then we cannot be harmed by them, because these feelings are in us and are us.

When we know that we are acting well, we are astonished by our own acting

—we might ask, from where do I know this? I have never experienced it before. The reaction to the atmosphere means to react to it. Personally we have the right to say we have no reaction to the awe of the cathedral, but as soon as we are actors, we must have it. For instance, if I am a cynical person, I will remain so, often on purpose, because in our everyday personality we are just as stiff as a chair. In our creative individuality there are both possibilities. There are limitless things there because we are able in our creative spirit to combine things which we cannot even think of combining in our everyday life. For instance, let us say I am a religious person and an atheist—it is difficult to imagine such a person but in this other realm there are both. Indescribable beauty of no time or space, everything together in the realm of *transformed feelings*.

What distinguishes these things from a cliché?

I think we can imagine cliches as follows: Clichés exist only in the personal feeling life, and not in the transformed feelings where there are no clichés because there is complete freedom. Clichés are necessary because we are very limited persons, so we appeal to them as the easiest way, but as soon as we can penetrate into the realm of transformed feelings we do not need them. Of course, when you speak of a religious person or an atheist, if you will consider your intellectual conception of them you will see that it is a cliché.

Our intellect is a series of subtle or crude clichés, but in our creative spirit are concepts of transformed imaginings, transformed feelings and will impulses. Since they are transformed and we have found an approach to them, and the whole method as I understand it is the way to open the door to this world of transformed things—then we do not need clichés. Of course, our body will force us to use clichés which are sitting here and there in us, but we have to gradually fight free of them.

It should be a continuous process, as opposed to clichés which are always fixed and stiff things.

Yes. The gesture is always a continuous process. Clichés are stiff things, while the other realm is one of endless, continuous process. By transformed I mean transformed to our life. For instance, you have experienced something very pleasant, and you are still very happy about it. It is not yet transformed, but you go to bed and forget it perhaps. Then suddenly you, as a person, find new abilities in you. Where do they come from? They come from this happiness, this joy.

Is it transformed because the emotion is different from what it was before?

TWO STATES OF CONSCIOUSNESS

It changed when it became unconscious. This process does not depend on us. Every moment something is disappearing and transforming. It transforms in the sense that we have become objective about it—we are free from it. When I am very tortured by someone or something, I am not objective about it—it is me, me, me. When I forget it, the same pain becomes richer and I am objective about it. I can use it in my part. The real good actor must act fully and completely, having laughter and tears and at the same time be so objective that you can absolutely see what your sister is doing in the first row of seats. That is real freedom on the stage.

When we are possessed by the part and almost kill our partners and break chairs, etc., then we are not free, and it is not art but hysterics. At one time in Russia we thought that if we were acting we must forget everything else. Of course, it was wrong. Then some of our actors came to the point where they discovered that real acting was when we could act and be filled with feelings, and yet be able to make jokes with our partners—*two consciousnesses.*

CHARACTERIZATION

I want to ask about characterization and where to find things for characterization. When you are searching for characteristic material, do you try to choose things from people you know well?

Of course, you can use persons around you as suggestions, but better still you can use your own imagination, and then you will get suggestions—a series of suggestions from which you can choose, or merge them, or combine them, and simultaneously you can observe your friends or enemies and choose from their characterizations.

I tried to choose a quality of a person whom I knew, in relation to a character, but what got in my way was my own feelings about the person. It was a quality of will which I did not like, but I felt it was right to use in a characterization, and in the psychological gesture of the character, but I could not free myself from my personal feelings about the person.

This is only a question of developing this objectivity I spoke about, but it will come after certain means have been applied. You will become more and more objective about it, and on the other hand, the power of concentration will lead you to become free from personal feelings. Then the moment will come when your personal connections will be less significant and will not disturb you.

You were speaking about the transformation taking place long after the thing may have happened. When you are portraying a part which is completely foreign to you, for instance, you must draw upon your conception of it and the picture of the part in the play. As an example: there was a play called Mulatto, *the premise of which was that the boy was a mulatto, but rebelled against it. One time a boy from Texas played the part with great racial prejudice—the lines can be motivated either way—but instead of subjectively placing himself in the author's hands, the actor played his own personal idea of it and ruined the play, but gave a very good performance.*

THE CREATIVE INDIVIDUALITY—
THE HIGHER INDIVIDUALITY

That is an interesting problem because it is just the problem of our creative individuality. Our creative individuality has a certain world outlook, and this world outlook—if it is the creative individuality and not your own political convictions—if it is the voice of your creative individuality, then it is the most valuable thing, your individual conception.

Perhaps this example you have given was not a very high example of the creative individuality, but for instance, if the actor becomes absolutely objective, it might seem theoretically that this objectivity increases to the highest degree, but will lose the individual point of view. But quite the opposite is true, because it is the world of the creative spirit, which is absolutely different from our usual conception of a human being. Therefore, the more objective we are as artists, the more freedom the individual has to interpret the character this way or that. The less objective we are, the more chained to our everyday feelings we are, and the less our creative individuality can speak.

From this mistake in approaching the play, or the part, from purely personal will impulses or ideas, comes the thought that I must produce Shakespeare's *Hamlet*—I cannot have any idea of his Hamlet, but only my conception of it. To have that is the only thing which the audience wants to see, whether it knows it or not. Because we appreciate all the old masters, not for the blue and the green colors and the figures, but because we see in Raphael that which we cannot find in Rembrandt.

COLLABORATION OF AUTHOR, ACTOR, AND DIRECTOR

Does the actor bear that relationship to the play? If so, where does the author come in?

It is a combination. Bernard Shaw is an author who has no idea of the theatre. He thinks that he alone exists in the whole world, and if he has imagined and written a line in a certain way, it must be done only that way. But strangely enough, he always interferes with the directing, and does such things! It is so tasteless, from the point of view of the theatre. Shaw has a concept of his play, the actor has another, and the director still another.

In the realm of the creative theatre nothing can be found which cannot be merged into another thing. For instance, if Bernard Shaw and the actor would merge their imaginations, Bernard Shaw would be grateful to the actor, because he would explain something to him. Just so with the actor. If the actor is open to Bernard Shaw, he will get so many inspirations from him, and the performance will be Bernard Shaw's interpretation, plus the actor's interpretation. But if one submits to the other, it is wrong.

If the actor is really using the *higher individuality*, the *creative individuality*, then he will need the author, and while accepting him, will transform him. Of course, we are all bound by our racial characteristics which influence our acting very much, but still there are always higher and higher points of view, and in this realm the higher it is the less it is connected with the binding racial characteristics.

We have spoken some days ago about the many gestures which foreigners make. But if I am acting an Englishman, I must use the English manner of moving my hands and arms. I must stop being a Russian and be free to perform an Englishman. But how can I get to this point? I must imagine the play long enough to get rid of my Russian reaction. It is not at all the question of substituting this hatred for some other kind of hatred, for example. No. I must look at the character in my imagination so long that it will be purified, and will become more and more artistic by the process of imaginging, which is art. Then the moment will come when you will be free from anything you have to take from below, and things will come from other sources and you will see that it is objectively true. You will understand this kind of objective hatred, for instance. Again we must appeal to this region of the transformed things.

That is why you say that an actor has to be a special kind of person, who can feel all these different things.

Every actor knows that there is a certain different manner of knowing things than the usual way. It has to be cultivated, so that it will become more important for the actor than the usual manner.

Ninth Class

The Psychological Gesture

December 5, 1941

GESTURE—ACTION—MOVEMENT

We must plunge again into the question of gesture in order to finish it. I am going to try again to explain what I mean under the possibility of interpreting everything which is going on while we are rehearsing on the stage, as *gesture*, or *action*, or *movement*. Whichever term we wish to use. Under the term gesture, perhaps we will understand everything I am going to tell you. Everything can be turned into a gesture with qualities. That seems to me the most simple way to approach the play, and the actor's nature. With one stroke we will kill two birds.

THE PSYCHOLOGICAL GESTURE

If we try to imagine and try to see what the human language has created for describing certain psychological states, we shall find that what we consider a purely psychological state of mind, or of the human soul—which has nothing to do with gesture—is actually described in our human language as gesture. For instance, we say, "To draw a conclusion." This is a concrete gesture of drawing. Actually, the language betrays all the gestures which the human soul does in "drawing a conclusion."

We must be brave enough to imagine and to produce even physically the gesture of drawing something in the way that we are drawing a conclusion. Then, if we are able to draw with our hands through the air above, let us say, then in that gesture we will understand more things about the human psychology, and acting, than if we tried to think it out. That is a characteristic of human psychology.

If there is a gesture to draw, and we can use any quality—imagine a character in a play who draws a conclusion. We can rehearse the process of drawing a conclusion by choosing the gesture—let us say the gesture is like that and the quality is "thoughtfully." Or we can draw a conclusion "slyly." The gesture will tell me much more about the psychology of the character, than if I were to sit and *think* about how a character draws his conclusion. Of course, I don't mean that we have to act this preparatory gesture. It is a means of approaching the scene, and the character, and the play, and it is easier than any other way.

Let us take another example, "To break one's thought"—we have only to find what kind of breaking takes place in the psychology of a person. It can be broken in different ways, with different qualities—all things are possible. Or let us take, "To delve into the problem." We can get to the point at which all these gestures will become an obvious thing to the actor's mind and soul. Then the actor will see that from whatever side he approaches the problem of preparing his part, everything awakens in him the desire to make a preparatory gesture, and in this case atmosphere can be used.

For instance, the atmosphere of "calm expectation" can be experienced as a gesture. Therefore, the atmosphere is always a gesture. Let us take another atmosphere—our famous cathedral "awe." Can we not have a gesture for this awe? You will not find any atmosphere which cannot be turned into the actor's language, which is gesture. We have gestures in all human psychology. We have atmosphere as gesture.

The objective can also be a gesture. The objective is something we want to get or to accomplish, and the easiest way to experience it is by doing a gesture. For instance, I have the objective, "I want to persuade you that it is so." It is quite clear intellectually, but for the actor to persuade, it means intellectually nothing. But the gesture is an absolutely free field for expressing this, and there is an endless variety of gestures. We can take radiation as another point. I can "radiate my admiration" in any number of ways.

We can take any point of the method and turn it into a gesture. While rehearsing, we must turn it into a physical gesture, using our whole body. What for? When we want to live, or while we are living the full life, we cannot do it as human beings without somehow having our whole body active. If I sincerely implore someone to do something—whether I move physically or not—inwardly I can only implore really fully if I follow and experience when my whole body and being is as if permeated by streams which are going on in me, so that each point in my body is complete. Then it is what we may call fully and completely alive.

LIFE AND DEATH IN THE THEATRE

That does not mean that I have to make the gestures obviously, but the streams have to be there if I am imploring someone so completely. Otherwise I will be a crippled human being, which is actually what the whole of humanity is at the present time. Even the foreigners who move their hands and arms and bodies very much are also half dead. In the modern theatre, when we come on the stage, we bring with us this death. This is true everywhere, in all countries. We not only bring this death on the stage, but, in trying to avoid using our whole being, we become still more dead because we think stage business is speaking the author's words and having some red spots on our cheeks. Therefore, we have killed the rest of our abilities.

I am speaking in general, of course, because there are marvelous actors in all countries who are not killing, but are increasing their life on the stage. But the theatre in general has gone down because of the loss of this life. Our task is to find this life again, because what the theatre needs is not decreased life, but increased life. The instrument we play before the audience is ourselves, so we cannot increase our life as actors other than in ourselves. Therefore, this gesture which occupies the whole body and being, is the way to increase this life, perhaps after a long time of exercising, until our nature responds.

To increase our own life of the stage means to be able to see everywhere—in the written words, in the events around us, and in our own psychology —gestures, gestures, and more gestures, but not states of mind. This is a very dangerous thing in the theatre, because the state of mind in the theatre is a fixed, dead, immovable psychology. But the state of mind which we must understand is one in which the inner movement goes on, and must not be understood as a fixed thing, but as an invisible psychological process going on in a certain definite way. "I am in a state of sorrow"—that means to produce a certain gesture, although it is called a state. It can be experienced—I can be sorrowful—in one physical gesture or another. I can produce this gesture physically or otherwise, when I am acting. The audience will respond to this better than if we imagine ourselves in a state of mind which is fixed and set.

CHARACTERIZATION—THE LANGUAGE OF GESTURES

For instance, if we take characterization, you will see that each character—however complicated it may be—is also a gesture. Let us say, for instance, that Don Quixote has a continuous gesture of one kind. Because of this gesture the actor will get an individual characterization, and each gesture will be different for each actor because of the individuality. Let us take Hamlet, and imagine that this gesture is my inner characterization. The gesture for Horatio would be quite different, and so would the gesture for Claudius, who is always lying in a complicated way, but he pretends to be open, and this will give us another gesture.

As directors, we can imagine the whole scene as one gesture. We can agree upon the gesture with the group of actors who are working in the scene, and produce it in accordance with the all-embracing gesture which leads and inspires them. For instance, in the "Mouse Trap" scene in *Hamlet*, we can make a certain gesture in which all the preparation and qualities reach a certain conclusion and are resolved. If actors love this psychological gesture, they will have immediately a purely actor's approach and conception for this or any scene. It will not be a philosophical or psychological approach, but it will be an actor's approach, whether the gesture is done inwardly or outwardly. Therefore, the very best thing we actors can have is *the language of gestures*.

If you ask me whether the "Mouse Trap" scene is really so simple, I would say that for the beginning it must be simple, otherwise we are compelled to walk through this labyrinth of intellectual interpretation—then we are lost. Great actors whom I have met in my life have become lost by analyzing their parts. They lose their time and energy, and become disgusted with the part before they start to act, because they don't know that there is the possibility of approaching the most complicated part by the most simple means of the gesture.

At the beginning it may seem complicated, but when we get this gesture and begin to love it, and experience it, and use it, then we shall see that this gesture is like a magnet which attracts so many things of a more complicated kind, through our psychology. They will be our individual things, not what has been written about the part—that is not important—what is important is to know what the actor feels. That is a principle which is important for all actors.

If we are producing these gestures, then we are accumulating, like a magnet, all the big and small particles which are coming to us, because we are occupied. Here again is another psychological trick. Our consciousness is occupied in these gestures, therefore, our talent is freed to such an extent that it will not remain silent, but will speak immediately as soon as we do not sit upon it and squeeze it out. The talent can show, do, demonstrate, produce. When we do the gesture many times, we will suddenly see something. It must come of itself. That is the whole secret. It cannot be squeezed out of us by reading books and critiques, or by using our own intellectual ability to analyze things which should not be analyzed.

When the actor gets the part, if he is conscientious, he starts to analyze it. It is a great illusion. Our art is quite the opposite—it is a synthesis. It is the *process of synthesizing* and *not of analyzing*. What do we have to analyze? What we have in our soul, in our creative imagination? There is nothing to be analyzed or dissected. It is a great illusion which actors have, hoping to get through their work more easily. It is the wrong way. The right way, as I understand it, is to synthesize everything which our soul, our super-consciousness, our creative individuality—call it what you like—can prompt us, being influenced by something, absolutely intuitively created, as the simplest and the first bell which we ring, and this is the gesture.

That is the first sign which I send to my creative individuality, and in producing this gesture I am waiting, and the synthesis takes place—all the things which my talent needs come by themselves from this simple gesture. If we are patient enough, and want to economize time, and to remain actors and not scientists, then this gesture will soon give us so many things that the whole character of Don Quixote, including his speech, his inner characterization, etc., will grow before our eyes and our imagination—our mind's eye—and in our inner emotional life. It will take the will and create itself. Our business is only to send the message, "I am waiting," and the answer will come and Don Quixote is there. When you are ready, you can use everything.

Perhaps it sounds like a purely egotistical business, but actually it is not so. We have to be open to all the impressions which are coming to us during the rehearsals. We have to be open so that if I have a gesture for Don Quixote, I must adjust myself to my partner who is playing Sancho Panza, not by thinking but by including all the impressions around me in my imaginary subconscious. I look at my partners as if I see them in my dreams, and if Sancho Panza does something which appeals to me, I will immediately find the right reaction. So it is not an isolated work, and cannot be. When I have mentioned that when the part is ready, we can use everything around us for our character, this same process actually takes place not only from the very beginning when you first take the part, but it starts long before you are going to play the part. Your actor's nature is absorbing so many things out of the whole richness of the outer world . . . and when you meet your partners, it is not increasing your connection . . . only perhaps more obvious than before.

When we produce such gestures we kill our stiffness. For instance, let us suppose we take the text and find a happy modulation of the voice, then we become terribly stiff, but the moment we produce this gesture we are as free as newborn people, and we can change our gestures as we like. So the gesture is the most freeing thing, in comparison to all the other means known to the actor. In using the gesture, we have the greatest opportunity to receive everything which comes to us from our partners, and from the director and the author.

I understand that the gesture is not only a physical one, but a sort of symbol of the psychology. What is the process which goes on before you get the symbol or the gesture?

Your talent. If you are not an actor, then nothing can help. If you are an actor, it means that you have already known many of these things. Why do you want to act Othello? Because you know it inwardly. Otherwise it would be a strange thing, like flying to the moon. People who are deprived of talent don't understand anything, either by looking or producing.

If I approach Macbeth from the point of view of the gesture, instead of analyzing his character, and I find that he is very weak even if he is a very strong man, would that be an intellectual approach? How would I think of him as a gesture?

First, you must produce the gesture just as you find it, then after you have done it many times, you can try to improve on it. Of course, the intellect will flirt with your gesture, which is all right. Then you can modify your gesture, and you will find different nuances. By creating the gesture you are exploring the part, deeper and deeper. Nothing is forgotten, only you must not let the intellect play the first violin. Your own experience will show you what manner of using the gesture you prefer—this is your free will. First eliminate the intellect, and start with the actor's means, which I call the *psychological gesture*.

This psychological gesture which you speak about, do you feel that it would create the form of the whole performance and would give unity to it? The performance could return at all times to this central gesture. It could symbolize the whole performance of the actor. Does the actor choose the gesture which is most telling for him?

If the gesture for the whole performance has been found, and it awakens the inner life of the actor, why change it? On the other hand, you can change your gesture hundreds of times if you desire.

I would like to speak of another aspect of the same thing. Something happened to me in a play called Rocket to the Moon. *I was very dissatisfied with my part up to the very day of the opening. I didn't feel right. It happened that on the day of the performance we were simply speaking the lines, and I heard a line which described my character I was playing, as being an orphan. For some reason this appealed to my imagination, and I saw a boy standing behind a window, looking out at a world of activity to which he did not belong. This was the pattern through his whole life. It appealed to me, and on the basis of that image I decided to play my part. It relaxed me just as you describe the gesture as doing. Is that something similar to what you are talking about? It seemed to illuminate the part for me, just as your psychological gesture does. Is it the same thing?*

THE ARCHETYPE

It is a different thing, but just as important as the psychological gesture. What happened to you, in my mind, is a very valuable thing. There is another thing in our actor's nature which might be called *the archetype*. It is something which embraces all things of the kind you mentioned. For instance, there are different lions running around in the desert—each is a lion, one bigger, one smaller, but there is a lion as an archetype. There is an *idea* of a lion which is the source of all lions. Call it what you want, but we must first create it.

Let us take the example of the triangle. How many kinds of triangles are there in the world? But when we speak of a triangle, we understand that it is not a square. We have the archetype of the triangle in our mind. One exercise is to try to imagine all kinds of triangles at once—all the geometrical things at once. You will *become* a triangle inside. This means to *get* to the archetype of the triangle, or the lion—all the lion's qualities combined together in the purest. All its roars, all its claws, all its movements are combined in one lion—*the* lion. Let us take the archetype of a king. We all know what a king is. We know that fairy tale kings are not real kings. How can we combine King Carol of Rumania with King Lear. Actually we can't, but as an archetype they are one thing. There is also a gesture for a king.

I think your image of the orphan behind the window was the voice of the archetype for all the characters of that kind which you were performing. At the moment it happens, accidentally, or by conscious work, that is the moment of the greatest happiness, and that is the moment when the part is there. For instance, once I was acting the role of Ivan the Terrible. I tried to get it by means of the archetype, and I found the image of a big bird flying with one wing broken. That was the archetype for me, and it gave me the part. Ivan the Terrible was an eagle, but a wounded one with a broken wing. When I penetrated the archetype, I knew that Ivan the Terrible, and the eagle with the broken wing, had one archetype.

So this is another way of finding the part, by trying to appeal to the archetype. There are no things which are without an archetype. Take a simple thing—the father. There are so many fathers in the world, and still there is *the* father. Of course, we can analyze this, but it is not necessary. The elder one who is very wise, he who leads, he who guides, he who sacrifices, etc. There are whole lists of qualities for the archetype of the father, or the son, or the king, or the princess, or death.

Do you see it in terms of a physical image? What would that be in the case of the father?

It depends on your individuality. My father is a very tall figure, with white hair. I don't know why, but it influences me. If it appeals to me, it can be the means to my archetype. Imagination takes part in it very strongly.

Perhaps I am mixed up, but it seems to me almost a cliché of a father. I think I would have to particularize the character of a father in a play.

Your father in a play is a character whom you have to portray with all your skill, and make it individual. But if you don't have the archetype of the father, your father will become a very small, dry, insignificant figure. If you produce my figure of the father, on the other hand, it may be only a stupid thing on the stage. But it affects me, and it gives me certain feelings—I feel what the father is. But the father whom I am portraying on the stage is absolutely an individual thing which is not the archetype, but it has been born *out* of the archetype, and has certain connections with it.

Does the play impose restrictions on the archetype conception?

The archetype does not take part visibly in my action—it is my own secret. It is the source from which I get confirmation for acting the father in the play—for enriching the role of the father in the play. Let us take the character of Joan of Arc. One may start the play having at one's disposal an actress with the physical body of Joan, and that will be a very small conception. But if the actress has in mind a certain archetype of the Madonna, or the Virgin, then her own body will become different because of this invisible richness of the conception of a virgin Joan of Arc. It will be a kind of "aura." It is only a question of an invisible richness or "aura" around the character.

In the process of working on a part, how do the two things stand in relation to each other—the gesture or the archetype?

OUR METHOD

It depends on the actor whether he uses one or the other, but if he really uses them, he will find that the archetype leads to the gesture, and the gesture to the archetype. All the points of the method which I have analyzed are one, if they are used. I have analyzed this method and have written it down, but when I have used it as an actor, then I experienced the whole method as one thing. When I thought of it, I put it in different categories, just as when speaking about it to you I have to be more analytical, because there is no other way under the circumstances. But I always suggest that you make use of it, having in mind all of its possibilities.

THE ARCHETYPE

Is it possible to use none? Let us say that a part is so close to the actor's talent that there will be thousands of images, and he may not need to know more than what the character is doing in the part, in order to play it fully?

If it were not so, then the method would never have been created.

I understand that an actor must always know what he is doing on the stage, but what I want to know is why I cried in one scene, and did not in the next. I have had to in-tellectualize it as best I could.

To understand what we are doing is absolutely necessary, and I have never tried to suggest that you must not understand what is going on. In fact, you will not be able not to understand! But there is another thing. To intellectually try to discover the next deeper level of the psychology of the character, by means of your intellect, that is just what psychologists do. But it is wrong for the actor, because our field is a different one. We can read books on psychology, but what use can we make of it for our art? It is not our realm. It is what I call the wrong kind of intellectual approach to the part for us. Of course, we might discover that when Hamlet asks Horatio, "Was the ghost pale?," it might mean that the ghost is pale because it is absolutely concentrated in his heart, which means that the father loves with his heart, while if the face is red, it shows that the blood comes from the heart and that means that, etc. etc. Of course, we can create such things, but it is useless for us. I mean that the intellectual approach to the part is one in which we try to dig deeper by means of *thinking*, instead of by making *gestures*, of finding the archetype, or other means.

What would be the archetype of Don Quixote? Would it be the same as the gesture?

If you see the archetype, you cannot avoid seeing the gesture which the archetype produces. While if you see the gesture, you will be able to see the image which embraces all the Don Quixotes. As given by Cervantes, it is almost the archetype itself.

Morris Carnovsky always had a great deal of interest in what he calls the Actor's Image. I remember working on a poem in his class. We understood the sense of meaning of the poem, of course, and then we tried to work from a central image. What effect the poem had on me imaginatively, and then, with that imagination, I had to say the poem. It seems to me that the gesture, or the archetype, is a further development of that idea, into the best realm for the actor, which is a physical one. To translate the image from the head or the heart, and to get it actually out.

If I may speak about Mr. Carnovsky's acting, I may say that it is very characteristic in the following sense. To my eyes he is always surrounded on the stage by tremendous waves—a big, powerful aura which is much bigger than he himself believes. How big he is on the stage, and how much space he takes. I seem to see everything in his acting—a clear objective as a gesture, a strong, strong atmosphere, very clear radiation, moving always definitely in a certain direction, with much "embroidery" inside, because he never acts too simply. When one looks at his acting with the mind's eye, then all these things are obvious. He always has the archetype. I get the impression—whether it is instigated by his acting or my own feelings—that his acting is the most complicated composition of gestures. It is the fullest acting and, for me, the most beautiful proof of the method.

It was the same experience when I heard and saw Chaliapin—if the actor is gifted, everything is there. But the question is whether any method is needed for the one who is so gifted. I believe that the more gifted one is, the more one needs the method to avoid accidents. If we are gifted, we may not find the character, we may not find the last thing which makes us so happy on the stage, and each day, each year, we will lose more and more our ability to be always spontaneous and creative, because of everything that is going on around us—machines, noise, war, Hitler, Stalin, Mussolini, and such things. They are killing our ability to be free on the stage, and our children will be to an even less degree in possession of their talents without any method.

THE THEATRE OF THE FUTURE

So the only way to preserve our talent is to work upon the method in order to get the technique, so we can save ourselves and our children. Then we will leave something to them—the method which we have gone through with all the difficulties, agreements and disagreements. We have to do this work, because without it, our children will not be able to create the method, they will be so overwhelmed by things which are going on around them.

After the war what will happen? There will be an explosion of joy, and then we will have catastrophe of economics and psychological depression. All these difficulties Churchill and Roosevelt know, but they hide them from us because they realize that we do not want to know what difficulties and dangers are awaiting us, after the war. Our children will meet all these phantoms, and they will not be able to create anything. This is the right moment for us, and if we do not do it, then the theatre will go down. Therefore, the method is needed for the cultivation of the theatre, not only for us, but for our children. And that is my real impulse for insisting upon the method wherever I am, because I am so afraid of the vision of what the theatre will become, knowing how beautiful it can be.

****

The gesture and the archetype are one thing—the gesture gives you the image, and the image gives the gesture.

What would happen if you had the archetype and the gesture, and you extended it to the point where it is symbolized into action? You have a gesture and an archetype which symbolizes your part. Instead of having just a gesture which is a form, instead of that you have a complete action. For instance, if the orphan opened the window and spat out of it. As a preparatory thing could you extend your imagination to take in such a thing?

If you are urged to do it, why not? But in the case of an actor such as Mr. Carnovsky, it would not need to be incorporated into an action—it only feeds him.

If you did such a thing, wouldn't it be changing the image? In my conception it was the image which persisted throughout the orphan's whole life, and illustrates everything he did. He was always the little boy looking out the window.

Whether you want to incorporate it or not is one thing, but as an image it is so feeding.

It seems to me the avenue for understanding the image and the psychological gesture and the archetype is the understanding of the body. The a, b, c of it is what you have illustrated when you concentrate the character in the knees, or in some part of the body. It is in the actor's learning how to concentrate his understanding of the part, that he finally comes to the understanding of the archetype.

Everything in the method is just the avenue—the elaborated body, the concentration, everything leads to the point where the talent feels it is freed. The body is a very important part of it. In our bodies there are so many enemies sitting which stop our creative process, very often in such secret ways that we do not know why we cannot act a certain part. But if the body is free, then forever I am free in this way. The bodily development is essential.

FIRST APPROACH TO THE PLAY—
THE ACTOR'S DREAMS OR INTUITION

I understand what you mean by the archetype and the gesture, and it is a very releasing thing. But when I have finished reading a play, I have always come to certain intellectual conclusions about it. I don't feel it would be right to negate this. In other words, could I come to an intellectual conclusion about the play before beginning to work for the archetype or the gesture? Should I understand completely what Hamlet represents before I begin?

From my point of view, it would be absolutely wrong. I would suggest something different. I do not mean to ask you to avoid understanding the play, but let us postpone it and let our actor's nature say its word first. Let us enjoy this business first, and when our dreams have broken through, it is not so dangerous to form intellectual conceptions about *Hamlet* or any play. It is never too late for that. When you are far enough in your childish movements and gestures, and have really enjoyed this period of your work, when you are ready with these free, childish, moving conceptions, then why not read about the play? Then you will take the intellectual things and carry them on the wings of your childish, moving conception, and will adjust them and recreate them to your belief in Hamlet and yourself.

When you read the play, the point is to leave yourself absolutely free to get the impression, and, out of that first impression, to use your gesture. Having read the play I get a certain impression from it, that is an intuitive, open thing out of which I must make the gesture. If, on the other hand, you were to read the play and then sit down and think and study about the social forces at work in it, or the psychological factor, then it would be impossible to get a spontaneous impression. It would have many false things in it, and would not have come from the immediate impulse and intuitive thing. It would be a different thing.

Would you use this up to the time when you are preparing the part, or is it just one of many devices?

It is again the question from which point you start. As I have told you, in comedies there is very little atmosphere, and the characters are very important, in drama characters and atmospheres are very important, and in tragedy atmosphere is everything and the character is not. It also depends upon your individual approach to the method.

I understand that the gesture or the archetype must come from the first impression, from the essence, but how can you find them unless you understand the character?

There is no contradiction. The archetype and the gesture are things which have to grow and develop. If you make such a gesture, and you find the archetype is the eagle with the broken wing, tomorrow you may find something else. You can dig deeper. Then you will see that you will not give away your archetypes or your gestures for anything in the world, because they will be part of your actor's nature, and all other things will be foreign to you.

You say that the actor makes the gesture from his first impression, and then he modifies it.

It becomes more and more complete.

Let us say you are the director, and you come to the first rehearsal. Would you tell us about the conflicts and struggles in the play, and would you tell us about the play from the director's point of view, or would you allow us to do all these other things?

It would all depend who the actors are. If the actors have no interest except to get the part, I would do just as all the other directors on Broadway must do. In two weeks the play would be ready, based on clichés from beginning to end. If we could work together, we would approach the play from certain other ways. If I got an ideal group of actors, I would approach it quite differently. I would perhaps start from rhythm. This ideal group of actors would understand, by receiving certain rhythmical indications, how to act. So it would depend upon the manner in which we meet.

We could use both the archetype and the gesture in our work on Broadway. We could use it privately, without the director ever knowing that we have heard of it.

But your partners perhaps would not accept it.

If you keep changing the gesture and archetype, do you come to the point where there is some set, fixed result?

If you have prepared your part based on clichés, nothing will be changed. But if you have prepared your part so that you are able to change everything and not fix anything, you will have the pleasure of changing your part, or the archetype, or the gesture through the whole period of acting. I will give you an example from my own life. When Vakhtangov was directing me in the play *Eric XIV*, neither of us knew about these things, but somehow we were both driving towards the archetype, or gesture. We found a complicated thing which was almost a gesture—we didn't know that it could be simplified to the point of gesture. Vakhtangov told me that if I had an imaginary circle on the floor and tried to go through it but could not, then it would be something of Eric. From this we found a certain form of gesture and shouting for the whole play.

When, for instance, you have found an archetype—complicated and noisy, etc.,—in time you will find a simpler form, and suddenly you will find a sly gesture which will speak the whole part for you. Simpler and more embracing, although it may seem nothing. That means you are growing. Another example:

When Stanislavsky was producing *The Inspector General*, he did not ever speak to me about gestures or archetypes, but he suggested the following psychological trick which was later the key to the part. He suggested that I start to catch things, and to drop them suddenly. So he gave me the key to the psychology of the Inspector General—he is nothing actually, but that is the whole beauty of the character. Something goes on senselessly. Just the same, one simple gesture can be found for the character of the Inspector General which includes everything.

A third example comes from *The Deluge*, and again it was before we knew of the psychological gesture or the archetype. Vakhtangov and I tried to find the most characteristic thing for Fraser. We found that the character had always to look or search for something he had lost. That was the whole psychology. He was lost inside of himself, but it could be simplified to the degree of the gesture. The gesture has to grow and develop, and you change it always.

There was another case with me. Again I was working with Vakhatangov. On the opening night of *The Deluge*, just before I stepped on the stage, I asked him what to do, as I was not happy in the part. He told me an indecent word which made me laugh, and this strange combination of being so on the alert, and then the sudden laughter did something to me unconsciously, so that I started to act in such a way as I had never done before. The character in the play was a Norwegian, but suddenly it became a Jew for me and remained a Jew forever.

All these things were accidents, but later I discovered what they meant. In the case of the last play I mentioned, it was a more or less dramatic part, and I took it very primitively, and had discarded all the humorous part of it so that it was unpleasant and straight. When the humor came accidentally through the indecent joke, these two spheres mixed together and the right thing came. Later on I found that there was a principle involved. If you are going to act tragedy, you must be very humorous, and if you are going to act vaudeville, you must act tragically. Inwardly you will be crying in the comedy, and laughing in the tragedy.

Tenth Class

Criticism of Scene by Peter Frye

December 8, 1941

THE ACTOR'S USE OF OUR METHOD

Michael Chekhov

I must say that I was very impressed by the scene. I don't wish to analyze, but in view of our work here I will try. First of all, I will try to analyze from the point of view we have spoken about. It was very interesting, to my mind, because there were four definite levels: 1) The person who speaks—the character. 2) Events about which the character speaks. 3) The atmosphere covering everything. 4) The mood of the person. The impression of these changeable and subtly interwoven things—this we seldom see. There was the atmosphere which didn't belong to the character, and the different mood of the character changed several times, although the atmosphere remained the same all the time. May I ask whether you did any work according to the method?

Peter Frye

I tried to use certain things. I tried to find the psychological gesture of the man, and to work with it. I gave him a center. It helped me tremendously to find different things to do with myself during the long narrative period. I tried to find colors and qualities.

Michael Chekhov

There was behind this little performance much more than was shown. You knew and felt much more, and gave us just a suggestion, which is always better than to show everything and try to pretend that there is more. It was in good taste, and rich enough by just touching upon it. If you had ever seen Chaliapin, you would realize that that was his ability—always to indicate, but not to show everything he had. That always makes a most fascinating impression, and keeps us spellbound.

Let us take another example—if you enter a cathedral and see different priests celebrating the mass, you will see that the whole secret is whether the priest *knows* more than he *does*, whether he believes and knows the spiritual events more than he is going to show—then it is strong. But when he does everything completely and fully, but nothing more, then you feel that he does not know what he is doing. I remember seeing a priest in Italy who was christening a child. The priest was happy and somewhere in his own soul he felt that he was not a priest at all, but was making a certain business and joking a little to justify this strange ceremony. He tried to persuade us, by means of these little jokes, that there was something more than he showed.

It can be taken as an absolute rule so that the part has to be elaborated with such care, and long intensity, so that as actors we will always be richer than the play requires. You will see that with "stars," what pleases the audience is that behind them there is something more which is so attractive and fascinating, and we can always develop this quality by digging deeper into the part.

RADIATION

There was another positive thing in this scene, and that was a very strong *radiation*. What was good about it was that the actor did not do anything outwardly to help it in the wrong way. You withdrew to such an extent that the outer means of expression became almost a pause. You could make it still more covered, and it would be a complete pause in outer action. In the real pause, the radiation becomes stronger than at any other time. May I ask you whether you had in mind to perform a Russian character? If you had not spoken some words to indicate this, I would have guessed that it was a Russian character. It was not a Russian character, but an American actor producing a Russian character. A most beautiful contradiction. It was a fine thing.

I felt that at the beginning, the actor was a little too glib, and the scene went along a little too smoothly for the man's feelings. Looking for the archetype, I felt that you did not have in mind the archetype of a person who has had this child. In my own experience, I saw my best friend die, and when I went to explain what had happened, the words came out, but in a way I was inarticulate. It was not so easily narrated. I felt the load on this man's shoulders, but somehow he explained it a little too easily. The inarticulateness of the eulogy was beautifully done in comparison with the beginning, which was just a little too glib.

Michael Chekhov

The actor managed the psychological gesture and the outer gesture very well. It was hidden and yet there.

I think Peter shoud do another piece of work in which the problems are such that he gives of himself completely.

Michael Chekhov

It is very good for us because it give us so much to discuss.

PSYCHOLOGICAL GESTURE

Peter Frye

I worked out the psychological gesture for myself, and then I didn't know whether to make it physical or not. I like the idea of it.

As I understand it, the psychological gesture is for the actor to work upon when he is working out a part. He uses it to help himself find the character. Does that mean that he incorporates the gesture into his performance?

Michael Chekhov

No. The psychological gesture is your own secret. It is the basis on which you stand, but how you act is quite a different thing. If you act without the psychological gesture, it may seem that you can act freely, without paying attention to the fact that it is shown outwardly or not. In almost all cases the psychological gesture must not be shown outwardly, because then it has more charm, more power.

Peter Frye

But you do have the choice of making it a physical gesture and showing it.

It still is the gesture which the actor finds for the character, which he can put into a physical gesture which will give him inspiration. Yet in its outward physical form the gesture might be a very crazy one, although for the actor it gives him a feeling of the character. But the audience might not like it at all.

Michael Chekhov

About the psychological gesture. For instance, if you look at different persons in your everyday life, you will see that each person has a psychological gesture, although the person does not know what it is. When we are acting on the stage, we cannot rely upon this natural kind of psychological gesture which every human being has. We have to create the psychological gesture, because the character is not the real being, until we give it life. Therefore, it is necessary because it is just what happens in the psychological life of every one of us. You will see that the simpler the character of the person is, the more primitive the psychological gesture is. For instance, the political agitator of a very cheap kind would produce a very crude gesture. In another example, the Englishman is a person filled with will which he has to cover even from himself. You can very often see a typical English gesture when an Englishman puts his fist in his palm. Very often, they use the same gesture. Italian people have a similar gesture, but up in the air, because they are much lighter. The gestures of the Latvians and Lithuanians are very small and short.

I don't believe in a psychological gesture in a psychological sense. The actor's desire is much richer and more emotional than just to convey an idea. In the case of the psychological gesture, you might choose a gesture which is more native to you as an actor, rather than the psychological gesture of the character.

Michael Chekhov

This decision should take place between the director and the actor—to share the information regarding the gesture and then the subconscious power will choose the gesture which will satisfy both. This talk which we are having about the gesture is a good example of how it should be done between the director and the actor.

Peter Frye

I found an entirely different gesture for myself, and perhaps I was too biased by my own gesture.

I agree with the criticism that has been made about Peter's scene. I criticize an actor on what he chooses to do.

Michael Chekhov

If you are the director, you have to criticize.

I would like to clear up the question of the difference between the actor's gesture, which grows out of the psychological gesture. For instance, in the part of Julie in Liliom, I thought there might be a great deal of feeling but with the inability to speak—a certain quality of shyness. As I understand it, the gesture is purely for the understanding of the part, so that everything the character does or speaks is colored by it. It is not something which can be used on the stage, but, on the other hand, there might be a part in which the character can very well use the psychological gesture. So it depends a great deal on the part itself. The gesture can sometimes be incorporated into the acting, but mostly it is a gesture which one experiences and keeps in mind when one performs.

Michael Chekhov

Yes. For instance, Don Quixote can use his strong gesture because he is such a primitive character, and to understand this quality he can use the gesture, and he would be looked upon as a child with white hair. It all depends on the character.

THE SPINE

Will the psychological gesture lead us to the spine?

Michael Chekhov

Yes. The spine holds the whole part, but sometimes we have the idea that the spine is stiff. The psychological gesture is always flexible. Everything will come together at one point. It is also very important to penetrate into the psychology of some person from the point of view of race or nationality, by listening to what the language conveys. For instance, let us take two extreme nationalities—English and Russian. In every sense they are opposite, and now look at the word they have for expressing oneself. The English is "I," and the Russian "Ya"—"ah" is opening everything, while "ee" is a very thin thing like an arrow. The Russian starts timidly, and then goes out into the whole universe, while the Englishman is quite the opposite, he looks around and then makes everything for himself . . .

For instance, if we read *Romeo and Juliet*, and listen to Romeo's speeches you will hear what sounds he uses, and then you will realize that Juliet uses quite different sounds. So you can even underline certain sounds which the character uses, and it can be turned into the psychological gesture. Of course, we find this only in such a genius as Shakespeare or Goethe—unconsciously, of course. You can underline certain sounds and you will see which character speaks them. But this is connected with speech, and in the speech method of Dr. Rudolph Steiner he explains this and it is very simply shown how the character arises out of the sounds.

Everything can be used for exploring and finding out what the psychological gesture of the character is. If we are observing someone walking—how they walk, what gestures they make—there is a psychological gesture hidden. We have to imagine the character on the stage—what sounds he speaks, what kind of voice he has, how he walks, what kind of pause he makes, etc. If we imagine all these things, then we will discover the psychological gesture of the character.

Peter Frye

You spoke in one class about the feeling of ease of an actor whose control of his actor's technique was so great that, while playing a very tragic scene, he was able to turn aside and make a witty remark. I used to have the other idea, that I had to be involved to the extent of breaking chairs, etc. When I was working on this part, which I adapted from a very sentimental story, and it was very sentimental at first, I was tremendously relieved. Since then I have tried to work at it, and although I feel myself to be in control of the character I have created, and I am observing it and taking everything in my stride, I still keep performing and sending out my character. At the same time, I don't feel easy or good or open, and I am wondering if that control takes that toll.

Michael Chekhov

It seems to me that you have not to control the first character interpretation, if in the first character you were crying and acting very fully. It was another character. You can have control over the first character just as over the second. But it seems to me that in the process you have changed the character. My impression is that it is this holding back one hundred percent in the wrong way which makes you tired. It is the manner of acting more than the style. If you are getting tired, then it is a sign that one little thing is wrong. But it was so slight, and so overwhelmed by good things, that it was no great fault. Such getting tired as you have described today comes always from . . . Go on with the sketch.

LAUGHTER—OBJECTIVITY

When we are laughing, we always step one step higher than we were before, because the ability to laugh is based, in the human psychology, on a previous life and previous experience which we have overcome. We are now higher than this previous experience. For instance, there are some things which offend one for one's whole life, and one is never able to overcome it. Suddenly the person feels that it no longer touches him, and that he has grown up one more step inwardly, and is now above this thing or things. This step higher means that we are able to laugh more than before, and the opposite is true that when we are able to laugh we are able to overcome certain weaknesses in our character, such as to be offended, etc.

To be able to laugh means to get a more objective point of view of oneself. If I laugh at others, it is not very beneficial for me, but if I laugh at myself, it means I am growing. The actor must have this ability. The more we can look objectively upon ourselves, the more our artistic abilities are flourishing, because the thing which keeps us contracted at times is our selfishness and our concern with ourselves; then we are slaves to our own personalities.

TWO STATES OF CONSCIOUSNESS

It is necessary to have two consciousnesses as Goethe had—one was always observing him, and the other was Goethe himself. The more we can do this, the more we develop the ability to laugh, and quite the opposite, if we are only laughing, without this other consciousness, we go on down to giggling, which gives nothing except that the brain becomes weak and the heart empty. To save laughter from this almost idiotic state of mind, we have to be tragic at the moment we begin to laugh, so that sorrow, at the moment we are laughing, makes the most human combination. Giggling kills our creative process and abilities, and we have to destroy it with seriousness which must be there simultaneously.

The tragic attitude towards life must be developed by very simple means. One has to look upon certain tragic events in life—simply concentrate on them, and see what they mean. For instance, what does it mean that Japan has attacked America with this sly business. If we really look at it and absolutely concentrate on it, we shall become tragic, because it is tragic. The ability to laugh we can also develop by trying to look at things which don't seem to be funny. For example, take a button and look at it long enough, and you will feel that you are going to laugh—it is a terribly humorous thing. These two abilities—to laugh about the button and to be saved from giggling by looking at Japan's behavior—and both are necessary for the actor.

SIGNIFICANCE

Everything on the stage must be significant—even if we are playing the most naturalistic play—everything must be done significantly. The actor must have inside him the feeling of significance at all times. I appeal to your instinctive feeling of significance because it is so near to the actor and so simple and will give to the actor, first of all, a very good style. Each of us can be significant only in his own individual way, and if we find the significance which suits us individually, then this significance will creep into our acting and will give us our own individual fine style. Another benefit will be that the audience will always follow us because if it sees something which is significantly expressed inwardly by the actor, the audience will follow him, and be with him, and help him.

Another important benefit is that when we develop this ability of significance, we shall lose the necessity to overcome the space in the theatre. Space will lose its wrong meaning for us almost immediately. For instance, if I look significantly to the left, the person sitting in the most remote part of the theatre will see, because even if they cannot actually see, the impression will be there, and the imagination of the audience has immediately grasped it because of this significance which they have seen. The smallest movement of the eye and face, or that the actor was pale or blushed, perhaps the audience could not actually see, but because it was done with significance, it seemed to be there. This significance is in the actor instictively. Animals move marvelously because of this instinct, even the little insect moves with natural pleasure. Just so, our instinctive significance must be awakened by simple exercises, and it will give great pleasure to the actor while he is on the stage.

EXERCISE

Sitting as you are, move your right hand and try to make it significant for yourself. That is the whole secret. We will experience our whole bodies differently because of this significance which is just as instinctive to us as is the animal's movement to it. Now look to the left significantly, and back again. Now look up and down in one movement, expressing this significance. It is the best means to attract the audience's attention. We are always looking for the audience's attention while on the stage, and when the audience does not look at us we are ill. Sometimes we try to use other means to attract the audience and waste our time, whereas we can use significance and the audience will look at us at once.

EXERCISE

Now let us make a quick movement and preserve the significance. While we are doing these exercises, we must overcome one thing, which is the tendency to become a little stiff and tense. Drop this and let it be a purely psychological state. On the one hand it may make one stiff, and on the other hand the significance can be so light, easy, and true that it carries us too far away and is too much, then immediately it breaks like a soap bubble. So we must find the correct type of significance without it becoming too bodily or too spiritual. Once I was scolding a person in my private life, and I made a very banal movement. I saw that the other person was so impressed by this action, because I was doing it significantly, and I lost the whole meaning of the thing! Now do an exercise by looking at each other significantly, and then lowering the eyes. Sometimes by ignoring a thing you make it significant, and sometimes we stress insignificant things to such an extent that they become significant in the wrong way.

Eleventh Class

Psychological Gesture

December 12, 1941

PSYCHOLOGICAL GESTURE

Take a certain gesture, such as "to grasp." Do it physically. Now do it only inwardly, remaining physically unmoved. As soon as we have developed this gesture, it becomes a certain "psychology," and that is what we want. Now on the basis of this gesture, which you will do inwardly, say the sentence, "Please, darling, tell me the truth." While speaking, produce the gesture inwardly. The more you will do these gestures, the more you will see that they suggest a certain kind of acting. They call up feelings, and emotions and will impulses. Now do them both together—the gesture and the sentence. Then drop the physical gesture and speak, having the gesture inside only.

Now imagine that your director has suggested a certain acting gesture, which has nothing to do with the psychological gesture. You can do the director's gesture and still have in it this psychological spine. The acting gesture and the psychological gesture do not contradict each other, and must not be the same.

Take another psychological gesture and listen to what goes on in your soul. Always exercise the gesture enough to be sure that it is there. In each actor's soul, it will be different, even if you are all doing the same gesture. Here we are really free if we start with the psychological gesture, because no one can know what is going on in your soul when you are doing the gesture. The audience will see you, which is the most precious thing on the stage. If you let your psychology be free, many nuances will come.

Use the psychological gesture as a springboard, and you will see that you are much richer than you imagine the gesture to be. The gesture must be exercised long enough to become a pleasant part of your psychology. It is always good to remember that although our physical body cannot go down into the earth or up to the sky, we can do so in our imaginary body. So the psychological gesture changes everything in space and time, because it is psychological.

Now, on the basis of the gesture, which has been rehearsed, let us take the actual business. You enter the room with your hands in your pockets, but in spite of this outwardly lazy, nonchalant manner, you have inwardly this same powerful gesture. This combination will make a very interesting psychology.

Let us imagine that we are playing *Hamlet*—we are all playing the part of King Claudius when he speaks the line, "How fares our Cousin Hamlet?" The director suggests that outwardly you have an absolutely free attitude, but inwardly you must produce the gesture of an outstretched hand with clenched fist, and eyes straight forward.

TWO LEVELS OF ACTING

Now let us imagine that Hamlet has another gesture—the gesture of drawing everything into himself continuously. Hamlet's psychological gesture is also to take only the things which are before him, but he tries to reach out as far as possible. It is a small, narrow section, but one which stretches over a long distance. Don't forget the legs and feet which do not have to move, but certain streams are warming them. Hamlet's head is down, and his eyes are looking forward. He says, "Excellent, i'faith." He stands quite calmly, but the whole inner activity is that of the gesture. Try to produce the inner gesture continuously, and then you can play with your outer gesture as you like. If there is the spine, the audience will get this second level which is always more interesting than the first level. The second level is always the psychological gesture.

TEMPO

The Queen's gesture will be one of closed eyes, the neck stretched, and as if parting a curtain with her hands. Here, let me make another point. If two persons are speaking together, one may be speaking in a very quick tempo while the other listens. The listener can listen in the same tempo or in a contradictory tempo, which will be much more interesting. There is always the possibility of at least two tempos. When we come to the work on rhythm, you will see what an enormous field there is for these things. They can be in two levels or in many levels.

Let us continue the exercise on the "Hamlet" scene. This time, let all the movements be quick, and the speeches slow. In this small scene many variations can be made. It can be quick speech and slow movements, etc. In order to be able to manage movements in different tempos than the speech, it is very good to do the following exercises.

STACCATO AND LEGATO MOVEMENTS

In staccato all the movements are sure and fixed. Our bodies actually do not obey us. We do things we are accustomed to do and usually don't notice them, but on the stage we find that our bodies do not obey us. We must be able to fix our bodies like stones, and if this ability is developed, it will give the actor's soul so many opportunities and possibilities to express things which we can only dream of now. The director will be able to ask more and more expressive things from his actors. Now let us consider the opposite pole: in legato all the movements are slow and flowing, nothing stops in our bodies, everything is like water, nothing is sharp. In this exercise we have to imagine that our movement goes on and streams and radiates out of our whole body. Not only is the physical body important in this exercise, but the imaginary things around and out of us are even more important.

It is important to be able to change immediately from one kind of existence to another on the stage, both in movements and in speech. Our speech depends very much on our ability to move. If we are awkward in our movements, we cannot speak well. So that in doing these movement exercises we are developing our speech as well. It is important in this exercise to develop the ability to express everything that is needed, without any preparation. Exercise by walking in legato movements to the chair, and imagine that when you touch it, the chair is white hot, and express it with sharp, staccato movements. This will awaken in you the ability to live in every kind of experience. It is like experiencing the life of two planets—Mars and Jupiter.

"TRICKS"

These things are not like absolute laws, nor are they clichés of any kind. They are things which are absolutely connected to human nature, but the more of such "tricks" we know, the more they can serve us, even if we don't apply them on the stage as such. If we know some "tricks," some day they will inspire us. For instance, let us suppose I want to persuade another or tell another something, if we act in the same tempo, it gives the impression that the understanding is not quite complete, but if the rhythms are different, the understanding seems to be there. Or if you have a moment on the stage when you wish to show the more emotional, moral side of the character, it is always good to face the audience. Whereas if you wish to show that you are thinking clever or sly things, or things to do with the intellect, it is better to show the profile.

137

Twelfth Class

The Future Theatre

December 15, 1941

You know, of course, that during the last third of the past century science—and later art—became very materialistic, and scientists at that time made certain statements telling us that everything was matter, and materialism. Of course, the beginning of the fifteenth century saw the rise of materialism, but the last third of the past century was the climax. The result of this is with us today. This materialistic point of view is what we are now living through.

What has happened to art and to the theatre is the following thing: we have lost the whole poetry around our art, and it has become a dry business. If we truly and sincerely consider ourselves while on the stage, we must admit that we feel our bodies and voices as the physical things which carry us to the audience. The whole theatre has become so materialistic for us as actors; our attitude towards ourselves, our bodies with voices, our approach to the new play is whether it appeals to our nerves, and if it does not appeal, it is of no value, and so on.

The theatre now is not solving any problems. It does not consider what the ethical, religious, or human problems are, or whether actors have any foresight. We are not interested in what shall happen. Everything is condensed to the present moment, and even more to the events of the present moment, and even more to certain events. It could not be more condensed, more stony than it is now.

THE FUTURE THEATRE

The future theatre cannot go along this way of condensing and making everything dry. There is no more space, no more themes for it. Everything is exhausted. The theatre must go the opposite way, which is to enlarge everything; the point of view, the means of expression, themes for plays, and, first of all, the kind of acting.

THE FUTURE ACTOR

The actor in the future must not only find another attitude towards his physical body and voice, but to his whole existence on the stage in the sense that the actor, as an artist, must, more than anyone else, enlarge his own being by the means of his profession. I mean the actor must enlarge himself in a very concrete way, even to having quite a different feeling in space. His kind of thinking must be different, his feelings must be of a different kind, his feeling of his body and voice, his attitude to the settings—all must be enlarged. The air around the theatre must be air. Let me formulate it in a few words.

"WHAT" AND "WHY": "HOW" IS THE MYSTERY OF ART

There is always a certain "what"—the play is "what," we have to deal with our parts as "what." In science everything is "what." There are two ways in this "what." One is leading to "why," and that is pure science. When we take a play and try to discover "why" the author has done this or that, we will never be able to act it. The other way is "how," and that is our way as actors.

For instance, if we know how to become jealous on the stage without knowing why, then we are artists. Under the heading of "how I believe the theatre of the future will develop," I would say that the more the materialistically-minded world forces us to go the way of "why," the less we are able to develop our abilities and talents. This "why" is very widespread in art in our present life. If you ask how can I know "how" if I don't know "why," I would say that it is a very materialistic question, because *"how" is the mystery of art*; it is the secret of the artist who always know "how" without any explanation, any proof, any analysis or psychological abilities. Quite simply the actor knows Hamlet, or Joan of Arc. Why? Because I am an actor. If we are unwilling to accept this point of view about "how"—because that is our life—then all the "whys" will never help us.

As an example, let us imagine we are talking with a brilliant actor about these things. He may say that he is not interested. Just let him express himself, his own "how," because he does not need our justifications. On the other hand, let us ask an absolutely ungifted actor about "why" and "how." Do you think it will help him? No, because he has no "how" in his soul. in both these extreme examples "why" is the materialistic approach to art which flamed in the last third of the past century, and from which we are suffering the results. We must make all possible mistakes in order to break all these boundaries to our professional work. "How" is our business, and "why" is the business of scientists.

OUR METHOD

Now let us look at our method. Everything in it has the tendency to break the boundaries of our bodies, our voices, and other abilities leading to this "how." For instance, the *atmosphere*, if correctly expressed, is nothing other than expanding our own being in the space around us, so that we become bodily less significant. With atmosphere something happens around me and in me, and my body becomes the instrument which receives suggestions from these things, and begins to obey these influences coming from the outside. So if we experience the atmosphere properly, it enlarges our being.

Let us look at the *objective*. The objective is my aim, my desire, it is what I want. Imagine it fulfilled. I am already out of my skin, as it were, out of my outer part of my being. I am somehow flying somewhere.

Or let us look at *radiation*, which means to give out everything I have inside. Again my body becomes larger and more artistic.

Preparation and sustaining is also something which precedes my hard bodily way, then follows it and goes on. It is again a way to enlarge the actor's nature.

The *psychological gesture* is purely a psychological thing, which leads us to ourselves as actors. Actually the psychological gesture is above theatre, and goes on further. Each gesture is the way to enlarge ourselves, and to break all these hard boundaries and obstacles which we have in our materialistic approach to ourselves.

THE ACTOR WILL DISCOVER THE SPIRITUAL THEATRE

When I try to imagine what the theatre can be and will be in the future (I speak neither in the mystical or religious sense at the moment), it will be a purely spiritual business in which the spirit of the human being will be rediscovered by artists. We artists and actors will write the psychology of a human being. The spirit will be concretely studied. It will not be a spirit "in general," but it will be a concrete tool, or means, which we will have to manage just as easily as any other means. The actor must know what it is, and how to take it and use it. This will happen to the spirit, and it will become again a very honorable thing when we know how to manage it, and understand how concrete and objective it can be for us. It can be much more expressive to our fellow man. I believe in the spiritual theatre, in the sense of concrete investigation of the spirit of the human being, but the investigation must be done by artists and actors, but not by scientists.

It is interesting to know what we are speaking about here some scientists are beginning to do. Already in many countries this new science grows gradually. Even in the field of mathematics, which seems to be absolutely stiff, there are new, flexible things which they are discovering and leading the culture, and other things become real art. Not long ago I visited a farm near Philadelphia based on this new approach. There they tackle these problems—they try to attach scientifically all the forces which are around the earth, the different influences of plants, and they plant their seeds in the ground at certain times. Certain plants are enemies and cannot be planted together. For instance, if there are two enemies with nothing between them, they will put a friendly plant there which will grow much more. The difference is so great, even for the eye. The earth becomes much richer, much more powerful. If they do not have these conflicts between enemies, then the earth becomes exhausted.

In each branch of science we have this new approach where many things are taken into consideration which seem, to the present science, nonsense. I am sure that to many actors in the world, what we are speaking about as a group is just nonsense. If they have a text and costumes, what else do they need? I knew a famous French actor whom I visited several times in his dressing room when he was playing different parts. I was shocked each time because he did not do anything with his make-up except to make two spots, one here and one there. So for him all these things would be mere nonsense.

Whatever points we take, each one is leading us out of ourselves. If you want to exercise these points, it would be good to remember that if it leads me out of myself, then I am on the right road.

CHARACTERIZATION

Today I want to approach the question of *characterization*, and explore it more carefully. First of all, let me say that it seems to me that all parts are characteristic ones. However, modern actors, in all countries, always try to act as much as possible as they would in everyday life, to kill every possibility of characterization in the part, and to adjust the part to themselves. Very often, we see actors acting themselves in all parts, without even trying to find out how one part can be different from another, which is quite the opposite approach. Modern actors, generally speaking, try to kill the characterization and make it so that the part is just as they are. This deprives us of the possibility of developing and showing to ourselves, and to each other, our "hows."

So it is a big mistake in the modern theatre to exclude characterization. Characters can be very fine, and very delicate, or very obvious, but it is only a question of dimension. Still, there are always certain possibilities for characterization. But how to approach it? Let us again start by looking at the wrong way first. If we accept characterization, or try to accept it, we may, first of all, rely on our physical body, just as it is, and try to contort it according to the idea which we have got from the part. Secondly, we may rely upon the costume and make-up. Or if the character is a fat person, we rely upon the padding, or if it is a tramp, we rely upon the torn clothes, etc. Everything from the outside. I exaggerate, of course, but only to make my point clear.

THE CENTER

Fortunately there is another way which is much better and much more appealing to our actor's nature, and much more satisfying to our instinct to create something out of it and then to see how the body, as a secondary thing, can adjust itself to this first, spiritual, imaginatively-created characterization. We have spoken about the imaginary center in our chest from which, if it is really experienced, we have got accustomed to the idea that we have a movable center from which everything is depending. We consider the normal person (without characterization) having the center in the chest, and everything is centered there.

Let us walk around with this center in our chest. It is the power which leads us forward. The only thing that is needed is that we pay a little attention to it, and gradually it will prompt us more and more to understand that we are sound, healthy, and well-formed—still without any characterization in the sense of the theatre. Let us sit down, paying a little attention to this center, and you will see how it supports and helps you.

One important thing must be considered. The idea of the center is imaginative but also concrete. It is artistically sound imagination to have this impulse from the center. Let us get up, being impelled by this center. Now move our hands and arms with the impulse coming from the center. Likewise, the impulse to lower the arms comes from the center—everything from the center. When we walk, our legs and feet get the impulse from this center in the most simple way, without any special effort. When we exercise in this way, we get the feeling that our legs are longer than we have experienced them before. The center gives the impression that our legs are longer, because they are connected with this imaginary center in our chest.

I have mentioned before that we have many locks in our bodies. For instance, our fingers can be so locked that they do not take part in our actions. All these locks can be opened by our understanding of the imaginary center, if it is developed until the whole body becomes free. This impulse from our chest will unlock all these things, and our bodies will become expressive, but if there is no source from which the streams can go through, our bad habits will eventually become so strong that we will have nothing to do but keep our hands in our pockets.

Now try to realize that the presence of the imaginary center in the chest is actually pure psychology, because having such a center makes one feel oneself differently. It is not a thing which is part of the actor's psychology. Every part of our body, our voice, reacts to these suggestions in the most subtle way. When we looks at ourselves in the mirror, we become different people. We want to see ourselves as we think we should be, but with the mirror it is not possible to avoid a certain selfishness. With the center it is quite different—we recognize the fact that there is such a thing as the psychological fact of this imaginary center.

Now let us move the center to the stomach, and see what psychology you will get from this. Try to walk with this center in your stomach, and listen to the new things which will come from this imaginary center. Let us say "Hello." It is already a characterization, but we have approached it not from the outer, materialistic, inflexible side, but from the purely actor's side where we are master—from our world of imagination, from our creative abilities, not from our body. Now move the center to the right shoulder and listen to what it tells you—no one knows how your nature will respond to this suggestion, but your talent will react immediately.

Follow any suggestions which may come from this—as soon as you displace your center, you will see that there is quite a natural desire in you, as an actor, to adjust your physical body somehow to this imaginary center. Now let us try to put the center in the forehead. The center can have different qualities, hot, cold, sparkling, etc. Try to make the center in the forehead contracted and cold, and follow the suggestions which will come from it. Now put the center about two feet above your head. Move about, speak to each other, sit down, get up, etc., paying attention to this possible change in psychology. Now let us dance, having the center two feet above our heads. Now put the center in the knees, and dance again.

This work of finding the center is absolutely free for the actor to try. Where is the center of Desdemona, for example? It is up to the actor to find out. How can he do it? Only in this way: we have to imagine the character which we are going to perform, in different situations in the play, and observe how it acts. We have to look at the character, first in our imagination, and see how the character acts, and what it experiences.

In our imagination we are somehow artistically clairvoyant, because we can see the feelings of the character we are going to perform, when we are imagining it. We can see King Claudius when he is praying—we see him fighting with these evil powers. We can imagine this figure, and his prayer only if we are clairvoyant in our imagination, and *see* what he feels.

When we take Desdemona, for instance, and see her acting and living in the world of the imagination, we see her utmost inner life, and if we put the question as to where her center is—in general or in a particular scene—the suggestion will come and we will know where her center is. If you see and hear Iago, being clairvoyant in your imagination, you will see where the center is. Because if you do not find the center first, you may be lost for a very long time, trying to grasp and incorporate in your body all the complicated and sometimes absolutely incalculable richnesses of the character. Othello, for instance, is a most complicated character if it is really imagined. There are so many things to be digested that we may become lost. The way to overcome this is first to find the center, and all the other things will follow more quickly afterwards. Without this we may be lost.

THE IMAGINARY BODY

When finding, through means of the imagination, where the center is—simultaneously with developing our imagination for a particular part or character—we can also imagine, or invent, as freely as the center all other parts of the body of the character. But before we touch our physical body—which is so stiff and full of habits that it makes us very uniform on the stage—let us imagine first the invisible body of the character. Let us say that we have found the center for the character in the diaphragm. Now we can just as easily imagine the arms and hands to be longer than they are—perhaps six inches longer. If we do not force our physical arms and hands—which will only make an unhealthy and bound impression—but let our imagination live with these longer arms and hands, we will see how the arms and hands will change of themselves, not because we force them to become longer, but they will give the *impression* that they are longer. If we try to stretch them, it will only give the impression that the actor is torturing himself, but if we rely upon the imaginative picture of these arms and hands, they will give the *impression* that they are longer.

In contrast, try to imagine that your imaginary body is six inches shorter than it really is. If you imagine it, you will see that you are so far from your own psychology, and that you have already plunged into another imaginary being, and you will have a different psychology, and will speak and move differently. Your whole temperament will change. Now, in addition, imagine that your right shoulder is higher than your left one. First imagine it, then let your physical body adjust itself, as it were, instantly to this imaginary body. The actor must be brave enough to say goodbye to his own stiff body, and follow the suggestions of the imaginary body. He must enlarge his being and make his being flexible. To answer the present materialistic age means that the actor must find other flexible, spiritual but concrete things.

Now let us change the imaginary body. The center is not in the chest, the imaginary body is one foot taller and the center is in the neck. Try to move, and you will see how the physical body will gradually want to merge with the imaginary body. Be aware, too, of the different psychology which comes from this imagination. In addition, imagine the body slim and slender, and the arms and hands longer, according to the tall, imaginary figure. Don't pay any attention to your physical body—it will adjust itself to the imagination and will be more accurate. Enjoy the imaginary body, and everything will come of itself. Now imagine that the fingers are long and tapered.

If you wish to use this means while preparing a part, I must remind you that imagination in general about the part would be necessary and simultaneous with your efforts to find out the right place for the center of the character. The legs and arms and feet and back and everything about the character must be imagined as well. Then try to speak words from the play, or improvise them quite freely, but one thing must be held back—don't attempt to force your physical body too early to imitate the imaginary body. Let it be lacking in expression at first—have patience.

When the imaginary body lives in you strongly enough, then the physical body will obey more easily and will imitate, as it were, this imaginary body. If you force your physical body too early, then the whole thing could go to pieces, because you might rely upon your physical body only, or repeat your old clichés. After certain experiences with the imaginary body and the center, you will find that almost at once your physical body will become like the imaginary one.

THE ACTOR'S BODY AND THE ACTOR'S ARTISTIC SOUL

We have to create our imaginary body in our fantasy. On the stage today the physical body is mostly the enemy of the actor. From the point of view of the theatre of the future, as I try to imagine it, everything will become more and more spiritualized, in the sense of concrete spirit. If our physical body remains undeveloped, it will become more our enemy than our friend. We must make an effort to separate our physical body, with its abilities and inabilities, from our artistic soul which is so rich in every one of us, so full of desires to create this and that. If we can separate our soul and our body for a moment in our thoughts, we will see what different worlds they are.

At the present time our creative soul is absolutely the slave of our body, and we cannot fulfill what we want to do. If we are able to incorporate, to act and fulfill one small part of our artistic dreams, we feel that we are victorious. But why not be one hundred percent victorious? It is possible, if on the one hand we overcome the materialistic conception of the theatre which sits in our whole being, and on the other hand we work upon our bodies. Even if we have been on the stage for years, the physical body is just as antagonistic to our creative spirit as it is to that of a student or an inexperienced actor.

There is no need to be ashamed of making these exercises, because it will do much more for our culture in the future than to repeat mistakes, and remain with our stiff physical bodies because we are ashamed of being students. We have such a beautiful future in the theatre, if such groups as this are brave enough to come to listen to someone who has something new to say. It is already a great step towards this culture.

Our bodies must be considered as being our enemies—they must be developed not only by means of our imagination, but purely physical exercises must be made to develop the body as such. Then from being an enemy, our body may become friendly. When this happens, it will be a great revelation to us, because we will see that many beautiful creative ideas, impulses, desires, and images have been forgotten, because the voice of our stiff body—from our youth until today—has always subconsciously prompted us not to try.

This intangible suggestion which we hear from our body must be corrected by developing our body, then our imagination will become free, and we will see things in our imagination and will be able to incorporate things which we cannot even imagine now, because we are always under the pressure of this intangible prompter, our physical body.

Here we come to the point that to develop our spirit is just as important as to develop our body. That is why I have suggested these staccato and legato exercises, because they are so simple, but they can overcome certain difficulties in our body. They must not be complicated. All these physical exercises must be as simple as possible. If we start with complicated exercises, our body will change them so that they will become comfortable. We must beat our body with simple, primitive means. One simple good blow of staccato is better than a more complicated thing.

FOUR QUALITIES OF MOVEMENT

Let us imagine that we have four kinds of movements. One of them we may call *molding*—whatever we are doing we mold the air around us with this movement. Let us approach the chair, moving in a molding manner. Then take the chair and place it in another spot, molding the air all the time. Then sit down on the chair. Everything must be done with this will which is molding everything around us, as if the air fills our whole being. It must not be strenuous. It is a purely psychological thing which fills our body. We must remember that the freer our bodies are the stronger they are. The will is something which does not need our muscles at all. Actually our will is not in us but around us—it is a psychological thing. The real will on the stage takes us from the outside. It is quite a different quality of will—much stronger, much lighter, much more persuasive. Light, easy bodies in which the will permeates and awakens us. When we are in a hurry, it is not the will but a nervous hysterical thing—to do things quickly, that is the will. We must not confuse these two things.

I want to say that none of the suggestions which I have to give you have anything to do with hypnotism. When trying to hypnotize another person, one must have such a strong imagination that you have done it. It is like the objective but turned on the other person. The will of one person has to overwhelm the other person. No means in our method ever lead to this. Hypnotism is old-fashioned now and it is seldom used, but psychoanalysis is used, which is still more dangerous. In our method, for instance, *radiation* means that I am giving myself whether you want to accept it or not.

Another kind of movement is *flying*. Do the same exercise as before—take the chair, move it, sit down, etc., experiencing the psychology of flying. Again, our body will get a good result from it if we do it properly. Try to do it continuously—the physical thing will stop, but our psychology will not stop—inwardly we must go on. These movements will break our psychological and physical boundaries. In flying you feel physically light and easy, and in *radiating* you will feel light and easy.

Thirteenth Class

The Imagination

December 19, 1941

THE IMAGINATION

Exercise taking the image of a flower and then moving around, talking and do-ing many different things, still holding to the image of the flower. If something on the stage is performed without previous or simultaneous imagination, then it is dry. But if, around your business, there is the "aura" of the imagination you have gone through, then there is the charm of art there.

Exercise getting up and taking a position, but do it in your imagination only. Then try to do it in reality. Then re-imagine it more strongly, and do it again.

Now have the image of a red scarf on the chair. Walk around, having a con-nection to the scarf all the time. If you feel the necessity to stop and study the image more carefully and closely in your imagination, that is just what is need-ed.

Is there a way of studying the thing objectively and subjectively?

If you are *thinking*, then it is not quite right, but if you are *imagining*, and *show-ing* first, then it is more correct. But it is not possible to distinguish. The series of exercises will distinguish so that the more *showing* you do the better.

Memory gives us the possibility of understanding how exact our imagination can be, but there is more freedom to create later on, and memory will not take so much part in it. First the imagination that we have exercised by means of the memory, then we will get the habit to be exact even by imagining a dragon, which we have never seen. If I know that in my imagination I have to *see* a dragon moving, then I have to able to see everything. The only aim is to train our imagination so that it will become absolutely concrete.

Then you should use your memory?

You should not use the memory which will take as much part in the exercise as it has to if you *imagine*. The more you are visualizing, the more right it is, and the more you are calculating, the more incorrect it is.

It is necessary to go through the physical process of imagining my body in motion, but it seems to me to put in my way an extra step by imagining myself outside myself. It complicated the problem for me.

It is very necessary to imagine one's own body. In the ideal case we have to have two experiences of ourselves, absolutely from outside, and at the same time absolutely aware of everything on the inside. This complete having oneself in one's control includes both things. I must know exactly how I look—it is painful, but it has to be. Then I can plunge into everything I wish. . . . Later on my instinct will govern and lead me so that all my short-comings and my positive attributes will be used in the right way.

During our first period of work with Stanislavsky, he stressed very much —during the first period of creating his method—that everything was from in-side and we must forget how we looked. It was a lopsided thing—we were very rich inside, but nothing came out because we didn't know how we looked. Then it was discovered that both things had to be developed; you are sure that you are inwardly rich, and you know how you look from the outside. So for a short period of time certain exercises may shock one, but it will pass.

When I attempted to get up I found I had to put my hands down to help me, and I was very unsatisfied with the picture I had developed.

That is just the thing which trains our imagination to be more and more exact.

Are we not supposed to have a feeling of the whole picture?

Of course.

Is it useful in this exercise to do much in relation to drawing and sculpture?

It can be very useful but from another point of view: to awaken a certain fire which is in us, but which is suppressed by our kind of living. We do not use our inner psychological fire. We can choose any piece of sculpture by Michael-angelo, and imagine it, and try to justify it in our imagination, and then we will realize what fire Michaelangelo had.

EXERCISE

Imagine a figure of a beggar leaning against a wall, and see only one thing—the figure is calm and the head and eyes are lowered. Now imagine the beggar look-ing up at you and begging with his eyes for alms. Imagine it and then incor-porate it. It is much finer and more imaginative because the beggar is no longer ourselves. We will see that our bodies are not flexible enough, and our imagina-tions are not active enough. Then we must imagine again the same thing and do it again. In this way we will train our bodies to become more flexible.

QUALITIES OF MOVEMENT—
MOLDING, FLOATING, FLYING, AND RADIATING

EXERCISE

We will do the following exercise on the basis of four qualities—*molding*, *floating*, *flying*, and *radiating*. March with the center in the chest, using the various qualities. The center in the chest makes our bodies beautiful from inside—the feeling that we are beautifully built. We are strong in our bodies. We are sound and healthy. We are large and tall. We are strong. We are active. We are full of activity and energy. We are able to fly. Close your eyes and imagine you are flying under the ceiling. We are light. We are healthy and strong. Our arms and hands are beautifully flexible and free. The center in our chest makes us strong, light, and free.

Fourteenth Class

Continuous Acting

December 29, 1941

We must at least *believe* that there is something going on in us continuously. Will this not increase in us our activities, our self-confidence, our ingenuity, our originality and our ability and desire to grow, day after day, week after week? Of course it will. If, on the other hand, we take the conception that we have sometimes to act when we get a job, but when we are not acting, we are passive and idle, that is not true. If the actor allows himself to believe for a moment that he is an idle person, it really kills something in him, and makes his abilities even smaller.

We must never stop. We are always going on, and if we *know* it, our inner life, and power, and beauty as artists will grow, will show itself, and we will use our means of expression better and stronger than if we are under the impression that sometimes we are active as artists, and sometimes we are not. If this seemingly simple and not very important idea is digested, you will see how much it will give you and disclose for you, and in yourself things may arise from within which you cannot get in any other way than to change your point of view, and get new conceptions about yourself and your art.

CONTINUOUS ACTING

This continuous acting can be done by means of exercising. Do you remember when we did gestures with qualities, and then we came to the moment when, after exercising the gestures and qualities, we went on acting and we realized that it could go on indefinitely? That is what our nature desires. Now let us start with some simple exercises and we will come to different things, but you will see that we come to the same idea, which is that we are constantly acting, and cannot do otherwise, because if we are actors, then we are actors.

IMPROVISATION

By this I am aiming at the process of *improvisation*. The illusion that we must fix things on the stage is one of the wrong ideas. Never. We can get many conditions and exact things from the director and author, but if we know certain things, we shall see that nothing can stop our ability to improvise, or deprive us of our freedom as actors.

EXERCISE

Make the following gesture: the left arm is behind the back, and the other hand on the chin. Now see what will be prompted psychologically by this gesture. Consider it as acting. Now, after you have fulfilled this gesture, make a little pause in which you do not move, but allow things to go on inside your actor's nature. After the pause, drop the hand and arm quickly, and then look up and drop the head. In this way, an unwritten play will be started.

THE ACTOR'S CREATIVE INDIVIDUALITY

Our constant actor's individuality is so rich and unique that we cannot imitate the director or ourselves if we rely upon our inner creative abilities. The cliché is an imitation of myself, or of some forgotten things which come from the past. Realize that in this little simple exercise which we have just done, our individualities had the opportunity to live and express themselves.

Now let us add a third thing to our simple exercise, which will be to cross the arms sharply across the chest, and take one step to the side.

THE ACTOR IS THE THEATRE

We can go on indefinitely, with nothing except our actor's nature, which is the basis for everything. So, when you have completed this little series of gestures, go on and see what will come from your actor's nature. The person who does not agree with the things we are speaking about and exploring together would say that they are without sense, but what you are doing now is really more sensible than anything else. It is clever and wise. I don't know what play it is that you are acting, but it is so attractive to watch because I follow you and am with you, and I see how your psychology grows, because it comes from the true source which is the only one—*the actor himself*.

The director, the stage designer, etc., are all accessories, but *the actor is the theatre*. The actor who believes in his constant ability to act. Then the play—even such plays as those of Shakespeare—is for the real, true actor only the pretext to express himself. We cannot express Shakespeare, because we do not know what he was aiming at; we can only express ourselves. Whoever the author is, we are always expressing ourselves. If we think we are expressing Bernard Shaw, for instance, we are wrong. We are expressing ourselves on the stage. We are always ourselves, or we don't act at all and are like puppets. If we are full of clichés or other disturbing things, then there is no theatre. But if we are real actors, we are acting ourselves, from our youth to our old age.

Therefore, it is important to have in mind that whatever the play, we are acting ourselves. If this idea is really digested, it will free us, even subconsciously. If we believe it, and get accustomed to it, and if it goes into the subconscious regions of our being, it comes back as freedom. I have seen many directors in other countries who did not know what to do with the actors after a few weeks of rehearsal. One director shouts to the actors to be free. How to be free? To be free means to rely upon our *ability to act constantly.*

Of course, there are things in every play which are "landmarks," as it were, and very often they are without anything which we are able to act continuously, so that we jump in a cowardly way from one landmark to the other. For instance, let us imagine that at one moment I am shooting someone and the next moment I am crying. If I am cowardly, there is nothing in between these two things. But if we really know in our subconscious that we are continuously acting, we can develop so many nuances in between the shooting moment and the crying moment. *How the actor will act, that is our mystery, our talent, our individuality.*

BRIDGES AND TRANSITIONS

Therefore, we may call this ability acting continuously and bravely, without any fear. If we, as actors, know that we are continuously acting, we can never feel that we do not know what to do next, because we can develop *bridges and transitions* between these two landmarks. Bridges and transitions between two given moments. Whether these bridges and transitions are short or long, they are the things which we are actually dreaming of. *How* we begin to cry, for instance, and what happens afterwards. *How* we begin to shoot, and what happens afterwards. Why we all instinctively anticipate the moment before we enter the stage, listening for our cue. It is the most beautiful moment. Instinctively, we want to develop this ability to act constantly, and with bridges and transitions everywhere.

All these landmarks are not as important as they seem to be. Of course, for such a dramatist as Bernard Shaw, only landmarks are important. He thinks that everything he has written, as soon as it appears on the stage, is a series of landmarks, and he kills the play. As a writer, he is a continuous one, but as a director, he kills the play.

EXERCISE

The first landmark will be that with a strong gesture and a stamp of the foot you will say "Yes," then leave it to your inner life to make the bridge and transition and go on to the other landmark, when you will say "no," with the quality of loving and a little ashamed, and with the gesture of your hand on your chest.

PERFORMING ARCHETYPAL PSYCHOLOGY, NOT PERSONAL FEELINGS

Please don't "spy" upon yourself while doing this exercise. Let me do that. Do it bravely and rely upon things in your actor's nature. At the moment when I take things from the other source and show *my anger, my feelings* on the stage, it is wrong. This personal thing on the stage must be killed in our art, and the way to kill it is to rely upon this source of transformed things, which we have experienced. That means to get to the source where we can continuously act, without any outer justification. As long as we rely upon this ability to act continuously, we are free from our wrong personal qualities.

While we are trying to awaken this ability to act continuously, we are safe and secure as actors, and are killing our personal things on the stage, which are always so offensive to the audience and to the actor himself. For instance, *performing* the quality of thoughtfulness is much stronger than the actual process of thinking, which is so personal. If I *perform* that I am standing there being very thoughtful, although I have nothing in my head, it is much more artistic and richer. Now, try to perform it. Then try to actually stand there and think.

Let us suppose I am playing a scene with another actor who says something to me, and I am really thinking of what he says. I am really thinking about it, am I not?

No. Not really thinking.

Suppose he says it in a different way.

That is "*how*," and you are absolutely free in that.

Then what is to prevent me from falling into subtle or obvious clichés? Patterns of behaviour, rather than the artistic impulse.

Nothing can prevent that. It depends upon the actor whether he is full of clichés or not. You can really think on the stage, and it can still be as much of a cliché.

As an original, individual being, I am likely to come out with some individual, original way of thinking. Therefore, it is likely to be more real and less of a cliché, is it not?

In the region of our subconscious there are many more patterns of performance than we will find if we are really thinking. First of all, when we are really thinking we have no time for performance. It will absorb everything, and we will become persons on the street, in a way, and it has nothing to do with art. It has nothing to do with being in touch with the depths of our subsconsciousness. If we feel we can lose ourselves if we have real thinking on the stage, and can substitute it with something which may appear as a cliché, it means only that we do not trust our subconscious, which can perform for us "thinking" in a thousand ways.

For instance, if you are acting Othello, and he is thinking, you have to *perform* it because, if you don't perform, then all the parts you will ever play will only become you. But if, through your imagination, you will find the way to your transformed personal life, to your subconscious, you will find many ways of performing "thinking," and you will know how Othello thinks, how Iago thinks, how Falstaff thinks. There are unlimited possibilities for performing, and you are free to choose.

Then what is to prevent me, as Othello, from thinking rather than indicating something senselessly. Why would it be wrong?

It is not wrong. The "sense" we are speaking about is the sense of your artistic "how." To kill Desdemona is an abstract thing, because as soon as you want to kill Desdemona on the stage, you have to find out—not in your everyday "street" life way—but artistically what it means for you, for anyone, to kill. Of course, it is different. Therefore, your killing of Desdemona will be really original only if you will find it in your subconscious, and the way to your subconscious is by all the means we have spoken about in our work. Simple concentration is already the means to find an original way of killing Desdemona. Imagination, psychological gesture—all these things are the same means.

You can compare this with Stanislavsky's justification. What do I do when the real life, my sense of truth, is not there? What do I do when I can't find continuous acting? Do I go back to justification?

If you are not able to act continuously, there can be two ways, as long as you do not exercise sufficiently to get this continuous life. So my first answer is for you to work along the lines which will give you this continuous acting life. If it is not there, then you can substitute it with whatever you want, with whatever means you know.

Then if you justify everything, you will act continuously?

In my experience, the actors who look as if they are thinking *but don't actually* think—the thinking which is not happening really, but which the spectator believes in—that is the kind of theatre which I have not liked. On the other hand, there is another kind of acting in which the thinking happened on the stage.

In the first case, if you didn't get the illusion that the person was thinking, that was the mistake of the actor who could not persuade you that he was thinking. In the second case, you could not even tell if he was acting.

I have looked into the technique of the two kinds of actors we are talking about. As a result, I believe that the actor who moved me was from the school in which the actor really tried to think on the stage, whereas the other was the highest degree of simulation.

I speak of a third thing. Not of the obvious, real thing, nor of the simulation, but of a third thing which is the *performing* of the real thing—not real thinking or the simulation of real thinking. There is another region in which we can penetrate, where we can get such performances which will teach us much more strongly than if we think on the stage, which is actually impossible. It is the question of a third dimension.

When I watch a person who is indicating what he is thinking, nothing actually happens.

For instance, someone asks you a question on the stage, and you have to think before you answer. You cannot have the *psychology* of a thinking person when actually thinking of something definite. Because as soon as you actually think it is lost time, and it is not art. The psychology of the thinking person is something quite different from a real concrete thinking person. This concrete thinking person seems to me to be wrong, because it is immediately out of the realm of art.

You are an artist, and you have already experienced this thinking, and you have a storage of thinking psychology, instead of rehearsing thinking at each rehearsal. I doubt very much that are actually thinking on the stage, even during the first rehearsal. You may have the illusion that you are, but you are not. The real thought does not allow anything to exist at the same moment. Even if you are thinking "I am going to buy a cigarette," if you are really thinking of it, you have no more space in your consciousness to think of anything else.

The thinking process is something which absorbs the whole human being, or it is nothing but floundering. It is dreaming in general. But as soon as you are thinking of the main idea of Schopenhauer, nothing else can be done simultaneously. Therefore, if it is real thinking you are speaking about, it cannot be done unless you forget that you are on the stage. The process of thinking excludes everything else.

For instance, you can be angry and you can watch yourself, but the moment you try to see yourself thinking you stop thinking and think of yourself. It is the only process which cannot be spied upon at the same time. So you have half the psychology of a thinking person, and half thoughts. But I suggest that you discard all this and have only and completely the psychology of a thinking person. Of course, you will have some thoughts and desires at the same time, but they will come from the other region. It is not simulation which is real life, but something a bit weaker. *Art is increased life,* therefore, it is quite the opposite thing. When we simulate something, we are weaker than the thing, but when we are acting, we are stronger than the thing we are performing. To simulate one can be paralyzed, but one cannot act being paralyzed inwardly. You have to have your own life, plus another life, plus ten lives as strong as your own.

That is something which troubled me when Peter Frye said that he could not project the thought. If he was concentrated on the thought, he could not be really acting.

Is that true for the feeling realm as well? When you gave the exercise, I tried to do it simply, as you suggested, but I didn't get much satisfaction from that. The second time I added things to it which made it more interesting.

If you do it ten times, you will create a whole story, and that is what we need. If it comes of itself because of the doing, then you have the right to accept it.

It didn't come because of the doing. I suggested certain things for myself.

Everything that arises in you is right.

But in relation to what we said about thinking, I am getting down into "street" things again. I should be able to do it without any thoughts or feelings which I have predetermined.

May I ask you whether you have an imaginary baby? No? Then it is all right. It was an imaginary baby. For instance, if the writer or author did not accept all such suggestions, he could never write anything. But it must not be *personal*—an imaginary baby is all right.

Let me tell you one more heresy. For instance, all the things we are doing on the stage, whether we are performing thinking, or willing, or doing things, they are all feelings from the beginning to end, because the whole art lies in the realm of feelings and not in the realm of thoughts at all, and actually not the will in the real sense of the word. One philospher has said, "Where is the will when we are doing something? It is a great illusion." For instance, I wish to pick up the chair. I think it is my will which I am expressing, but it has nothing to do with the will. The will is so hidden from us that we have nothing but a series of images or pictures of moving the chair. On the stage, and in everyday life, we are without any knowledge of the will. It must be the feeling of thinking, the psychology of thinking. *Feelings are the realm of art.* They must be absolutely concrete, but without any personal things.

If you try to keep it on that plane, is it not the same terms you are giving to the thinking process? Are these two things related to the archetype?

THE ARCHETYPE

Very much akin, because in our subconscious region archetypes are boiling in this kettle. Very often I have been asked how to avoid this everyday life. For instance, I am to act a very old man and I see someone on the street who has very interesting things which I want to imitate. Will that be the "street" approach? Of course not. I must take these old things and the posture and everything, but the point is where do I start? If you are empty, and you have no imagination and are just waiting for someone to imitate, it is wrong. But as soon as you have got this magic thing from your subconscious you have different eyes, and you can look at this old man, and it will not be of the "street." The old things will not be a simulation—they will be taken and transformed by the means of your subconscious, into the thing which we can use. It will be used as a piece of art. It will not be photographic. It will be a re-creation. We can use everything, but what actually is the motto? If it is the subconscious work, it is right, but if it is only a small personal thing, it is wrong. We must have the psychology of an artist, not a bourgeois.

RHYTHM

What part does rhythm play in this? If I am acting I must move in a certain way, but if I try to actually think I act outside of this rhythm.

Of course, rhythm is the highest point of everything, but we have to be absolutely sure that we can leave our personal things behind. Then we can be sure that we can perform rhythmical things, because it is the highest way of receiving and expressing things. But when you are thinking, you cannot feel the rhythm.

Perhaps there is a confusion of terms. When I was doing the exercise, I thought in general—I thought about thinking. How do I look when I think? But later I tried actually to think and it was very difficult to act it, because I did not have time to think of what I was doing, and that is not acting. Perhaps the thing you wnat us to do is not to not think, but to think with everything we have.

Right. The process of thinking, we may say, consists of two things. One is the thought itself, the content, and the other is the psychology of the person who is thinking. On the stage we have to have the psychology of a thinking person, but we don't need real thoughts. If you will analyze yourself on the stage while thinking, I am sure you will find that you have no thoughts in the sense that they are absorbing you completely. You are in a state of thoughtfulness, which is right. For instance, once I gave a certain actor the character of a philosopher. I could not get anything from this actor, because he did not know what the psychology of thinking was. He was not able to think at all in everyday life. That was a very strange case. Of course, we have to know how to think, then we will know how to *perform* thinking, without actually thinking.

On the stage very often we are put in such a position that when we are asked a question by our partner, we give a very profound answer. If we really had to think the whole problem through, we would not have the time to think of the answer. Therefore, the illusion is there and must be. I have noticed that when I am really thinking, someone may ask me why I am so idle. But when I am really floundering and doing nothing, they think I am thinking. Therefore, the *performance* of thinking makes more of an impression than the actual thinking does.

I find that if I have a scene with someone in which there is feeling and emotion—let us say I have to decide something—I will find that I listen as I talk or move, emotional questions will come into my being, like an inner dialogue. These are things which I would have defined as thoughts or thought-feelings. The questions are very much in the play, and very specific.

Then there is no contradiction. You are acting inwardly with feelings and everything. Perhaps I have made a mistake in speaking about thinking, which is really a philosophical thing. The real thinking which leads to certain things is a very painful process, but to perform a thinking person gives pleasure. What I want to point out is that actually we can perform everything—it is only a question from where we get it. If we are only thinking in general this is the worst kind of cliché, but if you have the substance behind it, even a cliché can be revived and made real.